ONE WORLD

TIM PRIESACK & TERRY TOMSCHA

REVISED • EDITION •

COURSEBOOK 2

PRENTICE HALL
EUROPE

London New York Toronto Sydney Tokyo Singapore Madrid Mexico City Munich Paris

Acknowledgements

The Publishers are grateful to the following for permission to reproduce photographs:

Ardea London Ltd p64 emu and wombat (Jean-Paul Ferrero), platypus (Hans Beste); British Tourist Authority p37 Glencoe Highlands; Bruce Colman Ltd p5 tern (Man Churchill), golden plover (Dr Eckart Pott), swallow and butterfly (Dennis Green), p64 kookaburra (Hans Reinhard); Copyright © 1997 by Universal City Studios, Inc. Courtesy of Universal Studios Publishing Rights. All Rights Reserved; Highland Mystery World p37 Museum, Seal Woman; The Hutchison Library p33 Amsterdam canal boat; The Kobal Collection p41 ET, John Barrymore Junior, John Barrymore Senior, Drew Barrymore, p83 Superman II, Indiana Jones and the Temple of Doom, The Mask, Batman; Mary Evans Picture Library p41 Maurice Barrymore; Reeve Photography Ltd p37 studio shot of kilt, whisky and shortbread; Rex Features Ltd p83 Alien, Back to the Future II, Star Wars; Steve Richards p15 currency; The Royal Mint p121 coins; Scottish Tourist Board p37 Loch Ness; Simmers of Hatton in Aberdeenshire p37 shortbread; Still Moving Picture Company p37 Clava Cairns; Telegraph Colour Library (cover) earth photo, two girls; Sheila White and Kevin McGeoghegan p55 cock in farmyard; Zefa Picture Library p5 cranes and reindeer, p67 general view of Gatwick Airport, check-in desk and departure board, p68 views of Cyprus, Sardinia and Corsica.

The authors would like to thank all those who helped in the preparation of this book. Special thanks to Maggie Aldhamland for her help, support and patience.

Published 1997 by
Prentice Hall Europe,
Campus 400, Maylands Avenue,
Hemel Hempstead, Herts
HP2 7EZ
A division of
Simon & Schuster International Group

First published 1991 by Cassell Publishers Ltd

Design by Linda Reed
Illustrations by Rodney Sutton, Taurus Graphics, Pan Tek Arts
Typesetting by Fakenham Photosetting Ltd, Fakenham, Norfolk
Printed and bound in Malta

British Library Cataloguing in Publication Data

Information available from the publisher on request.

ISBN 0–13–286865–2

2 3 4 5 01 00 99 98

Contents

Key to symbols used in the Coursebook

Listen/Listen and repeat

Language focus

Face to face

Over to you

Act out

Writing

Syllabus

	Grammar	Function	Vocabulary	Pronunciation	Activity
Unit 1					
a *Do you like pop music?*	verb *to be*: present tense, verb *to like*: present simple tense	identifying, asking about likes	hobbies, sports	/eɪ/ as in name	asking questions
b *Where does she come from?*	verbs *to live/come*: present simple	identifying and confirming	countries, nationalities	/ɪ/ as in give /aɪ/ as in life	writing from reading
c *Animal migration*	present simple tense	understanding points of compass	animals, points of compass, seasons	/ʌ/ as in summer	marking directions on map
d *Where did he go?*	past simple tense	asking about past	holidays	/ɪ/ as in did	matching words/ pictures, filling in form
Unit 2					
a *What sports do you play?*	present simple tense	asking where and when questions	sports and activities	/æ/ as in Saturday	conversation practice
b *How do I get there?*	present simple tense	asking and giving directions	street directions	/ɜː/ as in **turn**	following directions
c *The Teen Eye programmes*	present simple tense	understanding a sequence of events	words for television programmes	/e/ as in next	linking verbs/ sentences
d *Turn right at the post office*	present simple tense	asking and giving directions	street directions	/ɔː/ as in ball	giving and writing directions
Unit 3					
a *Do you ever go horse-riding?*	present simple tense + *ever*	asking about sports and activities	sports and hobbies	/əʊ/ as in **go**	conversation practice
b *How often do you play?*	adverbs of frequency	asking about frequency of activities	sports	/n/ as in **never**	conversation practice
c *Beatrix and her horse*	adverbs of frequency	describing habits	sports and horse-riding	silent r as in horse /hɔːs/	listening and reading
d *Strange brothers*	present simple tense, adverbs of frequency	asking and answering about frequency	sports and routines	/s/ as in **drinks**	filling in chart
Unit 4					
a *How much is it?*	present simple tense, *how much is it?*	asking about cost	currencies, numbers	/tʃ/ as in **cheap**	identifying currencies
b *You must stop!*	*must, mustn't*	finding out about highway code	highway code and street directions	/ɒ/ as in stop	conversation practice, dialogue building
c *I love my bike!*	*must, mustn't*	describing upkeep of bicycle	words about bicycles	/b/ as in **bell**	writing from reading
d *We must be quiet!*	*must, mustn't*, adverbs of frequency	asking about frequency	expressions of frequency	/əʊ/ as in **go** /eɪ/as in **play**	listening and identifying, filling in form
Unit 5 Language check	*Teen Eye on pets*	Revision	Topics: Pet shop routine, A visit to a zoo		
Unit 6					
a *What are you doing tonight?*	present continuous tense (as future)	asking about future actions	expressions about the future	/ŋ/ as in **doing**	conversation practice
b *How well can you swim?*	verb *can* (ability), adverbs of ability	asking about ability	sports and activities	/iː/ as in **speak** /ɪ/ as in **swim**	conversation practice
c *How long are you staying?*	present continuous tense (as future)	understanding sequence of future events	means of transport	/w/ as in **which**	asking about future actions

	Grammar	Function	Vocabulary	Pronunciation	Activity
d *Pedro's holiday*	past simple tense	asking about the past	tourism	/ɪd/ as in visit**ed** /d/ as in arriv**ed** /t/ as in watch**ed**	conversation practice
Unit 7 **a** *Did you have a good time?*	past simple tense, WH questions	asking about holidays	sounds animals make	/ɔ:/ as in d**aw**n /ɒ/ as in cl**o**ck	conversation practice
b *You speak French, don't you?*	question tags	asking for confirmation	expressions of ability	/θ/ as in **th**ink	identifying confirmation
c *He's going to score a goal!*	future form: *going to*	asking about future intentions	children's play, parties	/g/ as in **g**oal /k/ as in **c**oal	describing a picture
d *A day out*	future form: *going to*	understanding text about future	day trips	/ɑ:/ as in **ar**m	speaking from reading
Unit 8 **a** *Why don't we go to France?*	present simple tense	suggestions, making excuses	free time activities	/aɪ/ as in wh**y** /əʊ/ as in b**ow**	conversation practice
b *How far is it from here?*	present simple tense	asking about distance and time of journey	expressions of distance	/aʊ/ as in h**ow** /a:/ as in f**ar**	conversation practice
c *Do you think they play tennis?*	imperatives	understanding written instructions	sports	/u:/ as in d**o**	organising statistics
d *Dear Teacher*	present simple tense	asking about distance, time of journey	distance and means of transport	/ɪə/ as in d**ear**	letter writing, conversation practice
Unit 9 **a** *Would you like to go there?*	*would* for invitations	formal invitations	tourism in Amsterdam	/f/ as in **f**lower /v/ as in **v**isit	conversation practice
b *Do you want to play tennis?*	present simple tense	informal invitations	free time activities	/t/ as in **t**ennis	dialogue building
c *I'm afraid I can't come*	past simple tense	accepting and refusing invitations	party organisation	/tʃ/ as in wa**tch** /ʃ/ as in wa**sh**	letter writing, understanding invitations
d *Jane's party*	present simple tense	inviting	parties	/θ/ as in bir**th**day	dictation
Unit 10 Language check	*Teen Eye on the Highlands*	Revision	Topic: Scottish history and legends		
Unit 11 **a** *Where was your father born?*	verb *to be born*: past passive tense	asking about birth dates and places	family relationships	/ɔ:/ as in **a**ll	filling in family tree
b *My mother's father's brother!*	possessive nouns (genitives)	asking about family relationships	family relationships	/ð/ as in mo**th**er	conversation practice
c *A theatrical family*	verb *to be born*: past passive tense, past simple tense	understanding text	words about family	/dʒ/ as in **G**eor**ge**	filling in family tree
d *Who's who?*	past simple tense, past passive tense: *to be born*	giving and understanding information about family relationships	parties	/l/ as in **l**unch	conversation practice
Unit 12 **a** *There's not enough space*	*too . . ./not . . . enough*	expressing degree	people and places	/eə/ as in ch**air** /ɪə/ as in h**ere**	conversation practice
b *Each team has got a name*	distributives: *all, each, every*	understanding degree	schools	/ʒ/ as in televi**s**ion	understanding text
c *Is there much white paper?*	quantifiers: *much, many, a lot of*	differentiating countable and uncountable nouns and quantifiers	food and stationery	/p/ as in **p**a**p**er	conversation practice

	Grammar	Function	Vocabulary	Pronunciation	Activity
d *It's the highest mountain*	comparative and superlative adjectives	describing eating habits	food	/s/ as in sister /z/ as in eggs	conversation practice
Unit 19					
a *I'll be in Denmark*	future form: *will*	predicting the future	words about the future	/l/ as in will	read and sequence
b *When I'm twenty-five*	future form: *will*	personal predictions	the future	/əʊ/ as in won't /ɒ/ as in want	conversation practice
c *Will it rain in Birmingham?*	future form: *will*	predicting the weather	weather	/aʊ/ as in cloud	listen and check
d *You'll go to the mountains . . .*	future form: *will*	predicting the future	holidays	/j/ as in you	read and discuss

Unit 20 Language check *Teen Eye on food and drink* Revision Topics: Food and drink, The world in 2050

	Grammar	Function	Vocabulary	Pronunciation	Activity
Unit 21					
a *I went there to see my friend*	infinitive of purpose: *to* + verb	giving reasons for actions	tourism	/aɪ/ as in why	listen and answer
b *I was doing my homework*	interrupted past continuous tense	understanding time of events in past	school	/ŋ/ as in walking	conversation practice
c *Loch Ness*	interrupted past continuous tense	understanding recorded story	filming at Loch Ness	/eə/ as in where	listen and choose
d *Who saw the monster?*	interrupted past continuous tense	understanding written text	Loch Ness, school	regular past tense verb endings: /d/ /ɪd/ /t/	read and compare
Unit 22					
a *Have you ever played chess?*	present perfect tense + *ever*	talking about accidents	parts of body	/æ/ as in ankle /ɑː/ as in arm	read and label
b *Has he ever had measles?*	present perfect tense + *ever*	talking about health	childhood illnesses	/f/ as in cough	listen and sequence
c *Have you ever won a medal?*	present perfect tense + *ever*	discussing recent events	participles of common verbs	/eɪ/ as in play /ɪ/ as in win /iː/ as in be	class questionnaire
d *World class*	present perfect tense	describing past events	skiing and health	/e/ as in leg /ɪ/ as in his /iː/ as in he's	read and choose, conversation practice
Unit 23					
a *Have you seen it yet?*	present perfect tense + *yet/already*	discussing films seen	titles of films	/j/ as in yet	dialogue practice
b *I've been here for hours!*	present prefect tense + *for/since*	stating time of present perfect action	specified and non-specified time words	/ə/ as in yesterday	listen and choose
c *The classical guitar*	present perfect tense	understanding historical text	words about guitars	/k/ as in country	read and answer
d *Past and future*	present perfect tense/future form: *going to*, past tense	reviewing the recent past and discussing future plans	future plans	/ɜː/ as in first /ɑː/ as in fast	listen and write, conversation practice
Unit 24					
a *Has she been here recently?*	present perfect tense + *recently/* past simple tense + *ago*	discussing recent events	sports	/eɪ/ as in day	conversation practice
b *She's just gone home*	present perfect tense + *just*	discussing very recent events	post office	/ɒ/ as in gone	read and sequence
c *Where are you going to stay?*	future form: *going to*	discussing holidays	holidays	/w/ as in when /h/ as in how	listen and write
d *Time for a bath!*	present perfect tense/past simple tense	inventing conversation	hospitals	/ɜː/ as in work /ɔː/ as in walk	conversation practice

Unit 25 Language check *Teen Eye on the Olympic Games* Revision Topics: The Olympic Games, The Europe Quiz

Starter Unit Teen Eye Team

Fill in the missing information as you work through the units.

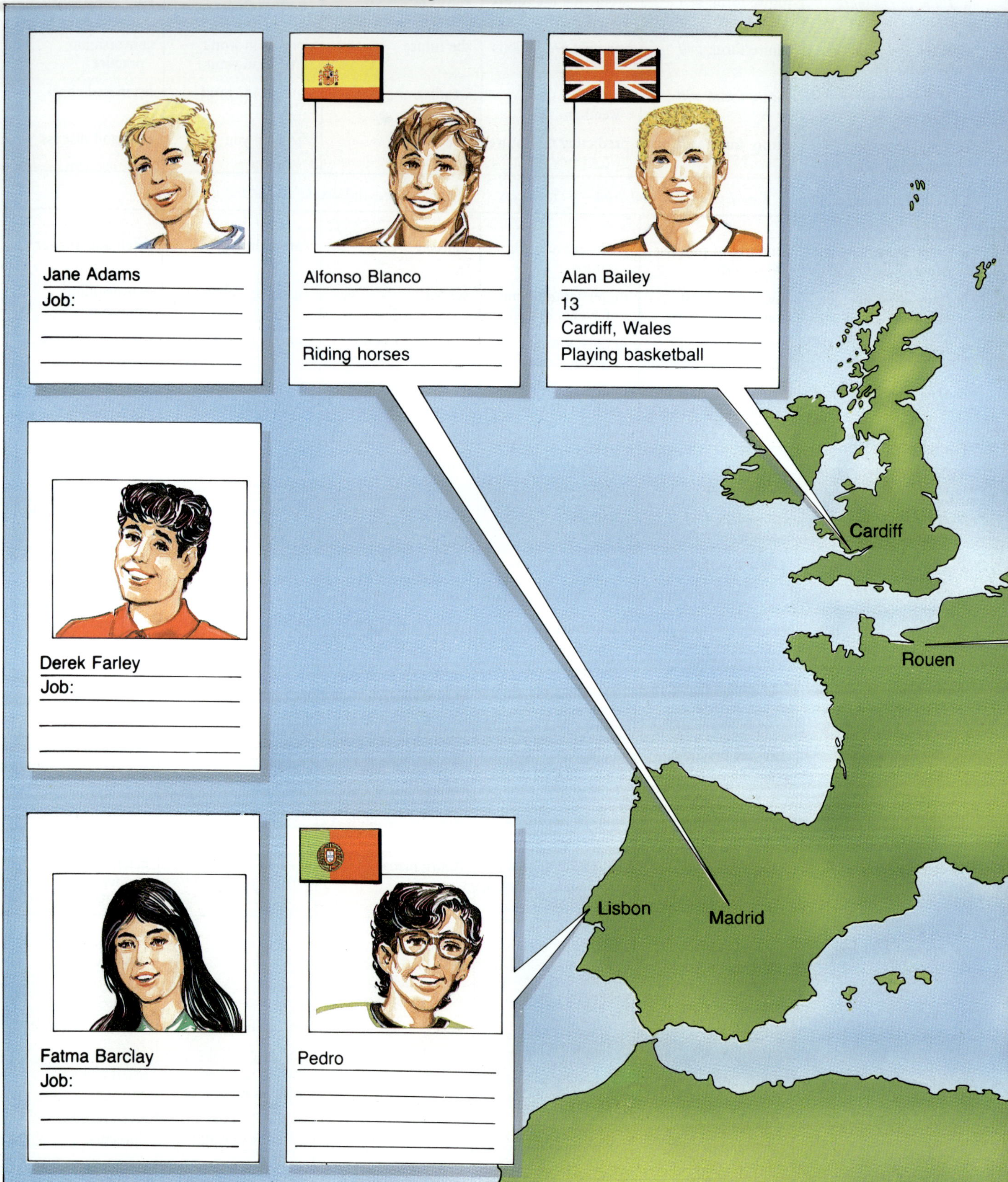

Starter Unit

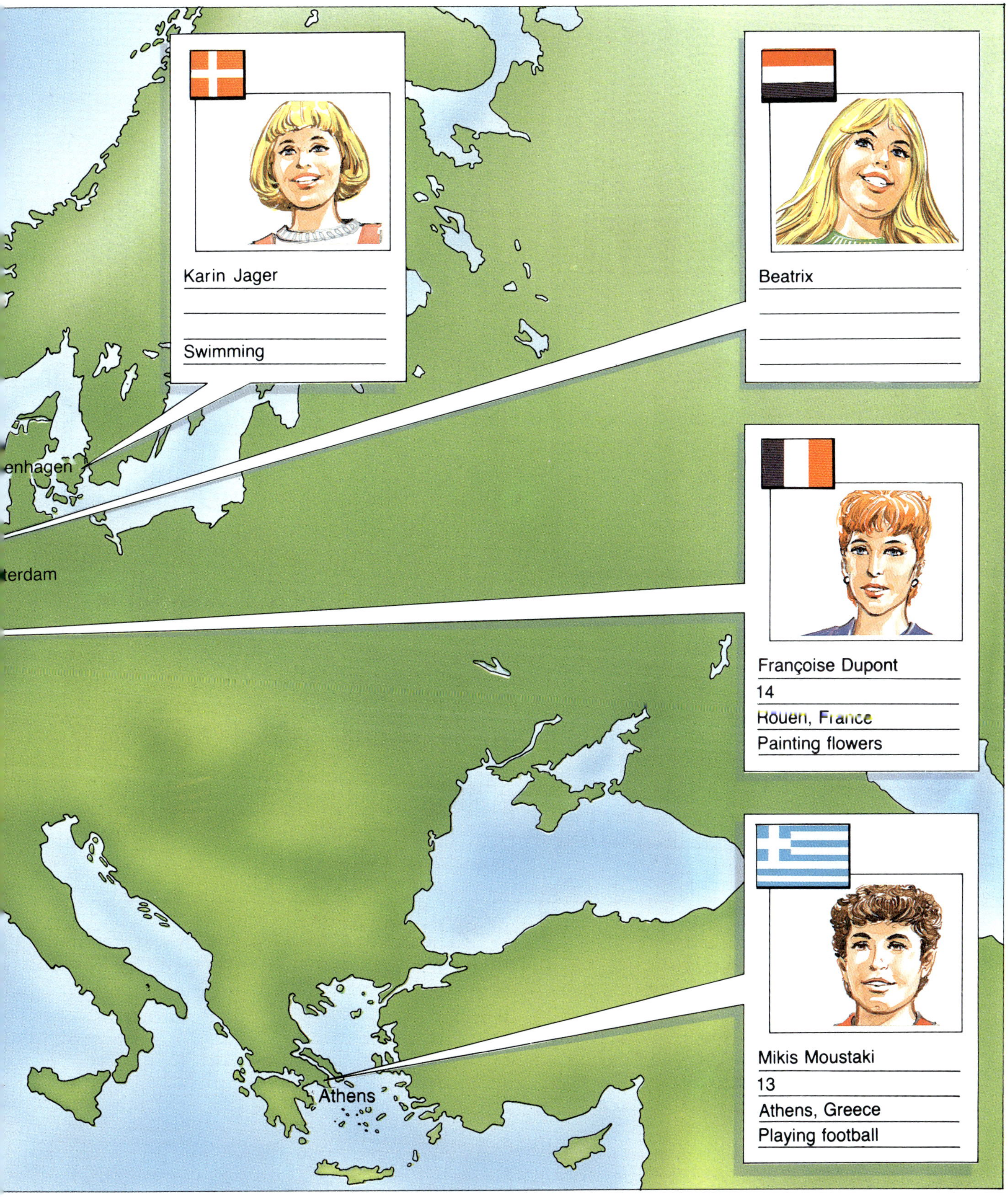

Unit 1a Do you like pop music?

1 *Meet the Teen Eye team. Listen to Fatma and match the names and jobs.*

Fatma Barclay	programme director
Jane Adams	producer
Derek Farley	programme co-ordinator

2 *Fatma is talking to Pedro. Listen and fill in the form.*

TEEN EYE

Member's Profile

First Name ....

Surname ....

Age ....

Nationality ....

Country ....

City ....

Favourite hobby ....

3 *Listen and repeat.*

What's your name?
What's your surname?
Can you spell that, please?
Where do you come from?
How old are you?
What's your favourite hobby?
Do you like pop music?

4 *Practise the dialogue. Use the information about Mikis, Alan and Françoise on pages 1 and 2.*

5 *In what way are these two questions different?*

Do you like pop music?
Do you like ice skating?

---

6 *Write these questions. Then decide which words are verbs, which words are nouns, and which words take* ***-ing***.

Do you like
- football? ...Do you like football?...
- walk? ...Do you like walking?...
- read? ....
- swim? ....
- classical music? ....
- volleyball? ....
- play volleyball? ....

7 *Make a list of eight activities you like doing. Then find some friends who also like doing these activities and fill in the other column.*

Activities	**Friends**
a.	....
b.	....
c.	....
d.	....
e.	....
f.	....
g.	....
h.	....

verb *to be*: present tense p 105, verb *to like*: present simple tense /eɪ/ name

Unit 1b Where does she come from?

1 *Listen to Françoise and Derek. Match the names, countries and cities.*

Alfonso	Denmark	Madrid
Karin	Spain	Copenhagen

2 *Listen again and tick (√)* ***True*** *or* ***False****. Correct the false statements.*

	True	False
a. Alfonso lives in Barcelona.	☐	☐
b. Alfonso is thirteen years old.	☐	☐
c. Karin lives in Copenhagen.	☐	☐
d. Karin is twelve years old.	☐	☐

3 *Listen to Françoise and Derek again. Fill in the information about Alfonso and Karin on pages 1 and 2.*

4 *Listen and repeat.*

Where does he come from?
He comes from Spain.
What nationality is she?
She's Danish.
Does she live in Copenhagen?
Yes, she does.
No, he doesn't.

5 *Look at the map on pages 1 and 2. Ask and answer about the country, city, age, nationality and favourite hobbies.*

6 *Read. Then write the questions or answers.*

Beatrix is Dutch. Her surname is Van Dunn.
She comes from Amsterdam, a city in the centre of the Netherlands. She is thirteen years old and she likes collecting postcards.

a. What..............................? She's Dutch.
b. ....? It's Van Dunn.
c. ....? She comes from Amsterdam.
d. ....Amsterdam? ....the Netherlands.
e. ....? She's thirteen.
f. ....? ....postcards.

7 *Ask a friend questions about his or her best friend. Find out the name, age, nationality, country, city and hobby.*

8 *Read. Then look at the information about Françoise on pages 1 and 2 and write correct sentences.*

Françoise's surname is Dupolt.
She's Swiss and she lives in Geneva. She's twelve years old and she likes painting animals.

Surname	Her surname isn't Dupolt. It's Dupont.
Age	....
Nationality	....
Country	....
City	....
Favourite hobby	....

9 *Ask a friend questions about the Teen Eye team.*

▶ *eg* Pedro/Lisbon
A: Does Pedro come from Lisbon?
B: Yes, he does.

a. Alan/Cardiff b. Françoise/Paris
c. Alfonso/Barcelona d. Mikis/Athens

verbs *to live*/*come*: present simple tense p 105 /ɪ/ give /aɪ/ life

Unit 1c Animal migration

Derek and Jane are reading about where animals migrate when the seasons change.

1 *Match the birds, insects and animals to the pictures.*

1. Crane (a tall bird)
2. Reindeer (a mammal)
3. Monarch butterfly (an insect)
4. Golden plover (a bird)
5. Swallow (a bird)
6. Arctic tern (a bird)

a. ☐

b. ☐

c. ☐

d. ☐ e. ☐

f. ☐

2 *Write the seasons.*

3 *Write the points of the compass.*

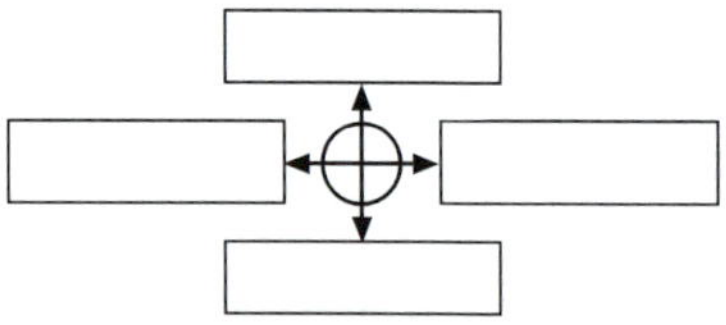

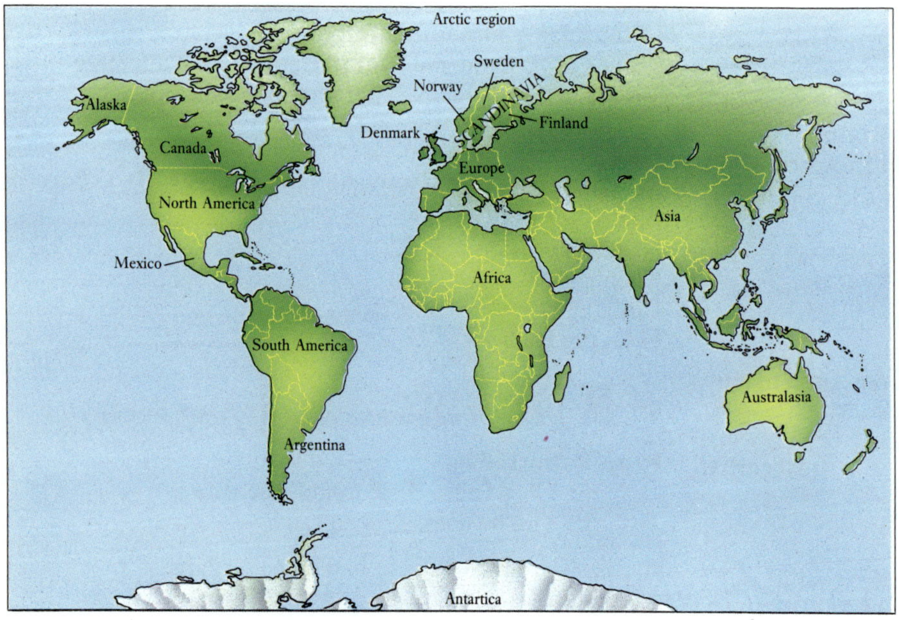

4 *Read. Then, on the map, mark the direction of migration of each bird, insect and animal and write the name.*

Migration

A lot of birds, insects and large animals move from country to country, from continent to continent during the year. Some move when the summer turns to winter, some move when there is no food to eat.

The beautiful cranes that live in Scandinavia fly south to Africa when the winter comes.

Monarch butterflies fly from Canada to Mexico when the cold weather arrives and then they return north for the summer.

The reindeer that live in Alaska move 900 kilometres to the south when it gets cold and there is no food for them.

Swallows from Europe migrate to central Africa and from North America to South America.

Golden plovers fly from Mexico to Argentina in three days – over 7,000 kilometres!

Arctic terns are very intelligent birds. They stay in the Arctic during the summer and when winter comes they migrate to the Antarctic, where summer is starting. They return to the Arctic when spring comes, and in this way they never see the winter!

5 *Read the text again and find all the verbs in the present tense.*

present simple tense p 105 /ʌ/ summer

Unit 1d Where did he go?

1 *Look at the pictures and complete the sentences.*

a. Where did Derek go for his .... holiday?

A Easter
B winter
C summer
D half-term

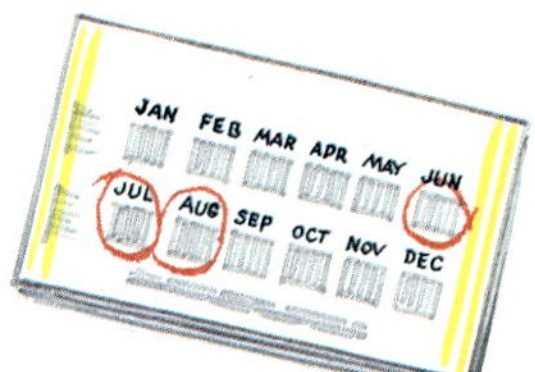

b. Derek went to ....

A Spain
B the beach
C the lake
D the mountains
E a city

c. He stayed ....

A with friends
B in a hotel
C with a family
D at a campsite

d. He travelled by ....

A train
B bus
C aeroplane
D car

e. He went with his ....

A family
B mother
C father
D friends

f. He stayed for two ....

A days
B weeks
C months

g. He returned .... August.

A at the beginning of
B at the end of
C in the middle of

2 *Answer these questions.*

Which tense is used in the sentences in Exercise 1?
Which verb is irregular?

3 *Write sentences about Derek's holiday. Start like this:*

Last summer Derek went on holiday to . . .

4 *Answer these questions. Then ask a friend about his or her last holiday. Finally, ask another friend about his or her friend's holiday.*

	Me	**Friend 1**	**Friend 2**
a. Where did you go for your last holiday?			
b. Where did you stay?			
c. How did you travel?			
d. Who did you go with?			
e. How long did you stay?			
f. When did you return?			

5 *Use your notes from the chart in Exercise 4 and write about one of your friends' holidays.*

Unit 1 *Chatterbox A*

Chatterbox B see page 93.

1 *Ask your friend questions about Derek and fill in the form.*

2 *Answer your friend's questions about Jane.*

First name	Derek	**First name**	Jane
Surname	....	**Surname**	Adams
Age	....	**Age**	25
Nationality	....	**Nationality**	Welsh
Country	....	**Country**	Wales
City	....	**City**	Swansea
Favourite hobby	....	**Favourite hobby**	Cooking Chinese food

past simple tense p 106 /ɪ/ did

Unit 2a What sports do you play?

1 *Match the sports or games with the pictures.*

a. ....

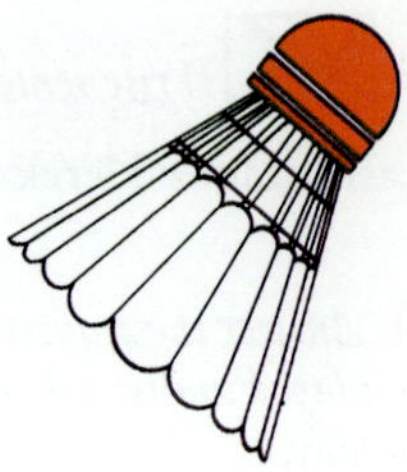

c. ....

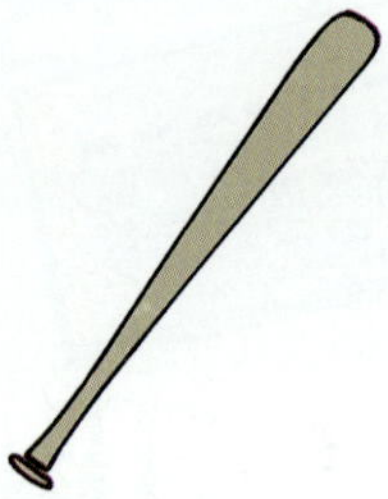

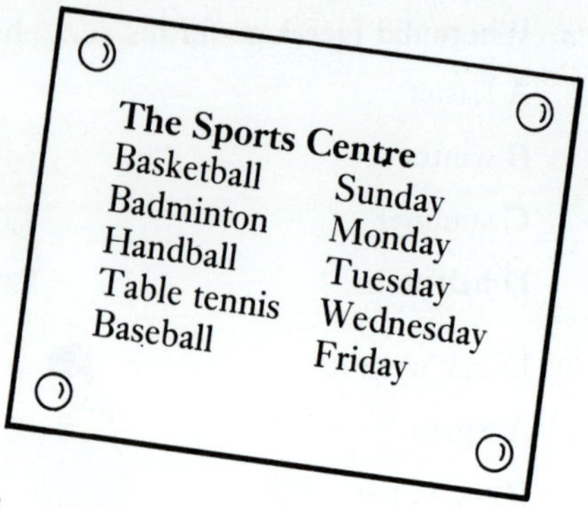

b. ....

d. ....

e. ....

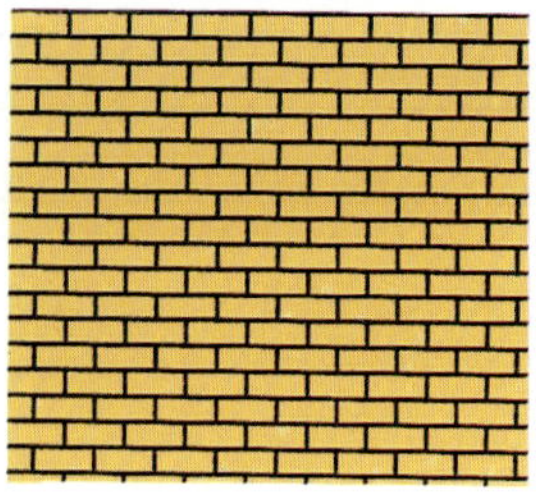

f. ....

g. ....

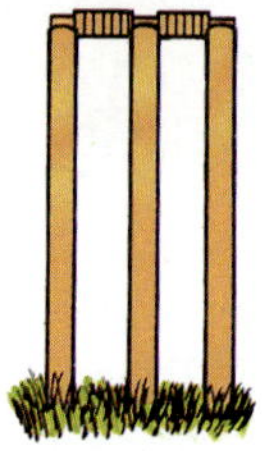

h. ....

i. ....

2 *Ask and answer. Use the sports and games in Exercise 1.*

► *eg* A: Do you like playing billiards?
B: Yes, I do./No, I don't.

3 *Listen and tick (√)* ***True*** *or* ***False****. Correct the false statements.*

	True	False
a. Mikis plays billiards on Saturday mornings.	☐	☐
b. Alan can't play billiards.	☐	☐
c. Mikis wants to play billiards with Alan.	☐	☐
d. Alan doesn't want to play billiards with Mikis.	☐	☐

4 *Listen and repeat.*

What do you do on Wednesday afternoons?
I play billiards.
Where do you play?
I play at St Mark's School.

5 *You and your partner are Mikis and Alan. Practise the dialogue. Use the sports, games and days in Exercise 1.*

6 *Write the sentences in the right order.*

a. What sports do you play?
b. On Saturdays.
c. Oh, I play tennis too. Where do you play?
d. Yes, of course. That's a great idea!
e. St Mark's School.
f. Oh lots. I play tennis, for instance.
g. Can I come with you next Saturday?
h. When do you play?

A: What sports do you play?
B: ....
A: ....
B: ....
A: ....
B: ....
A: ....
B: ....

7 *Make a list of sports or games you and your friend play. Then practise the dialogue in Exercise 6 using the sports and games on your list.*

present simple tense p 105

/æ/ Saturday

Unit 2b How do I get there?

1 *Match the words and the pictures.*

Go straight on   Turn right
Turn left   Stop

a. ....

b. ....

c. ....

d. ....

2 *Match the sentences and the maps.*

1. Take the first turning on the left.
2. Take the second turning on the right.
3. Go straight on and take the second turning on the left.
4. Go to the corner and turn right. Go straight on and take the second turning on the right.
5. Go over the crossroads and take the first turning on the right.

a.

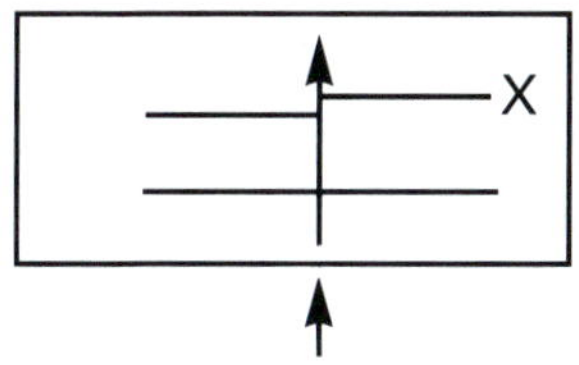

b.

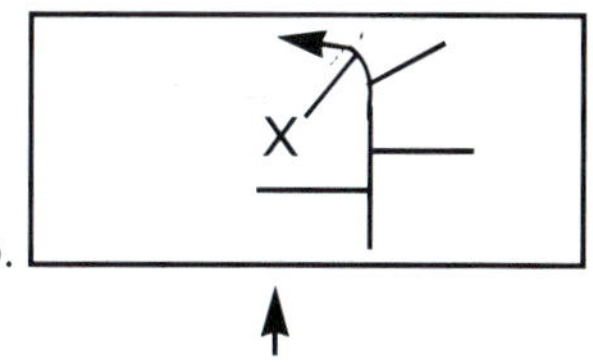

c.

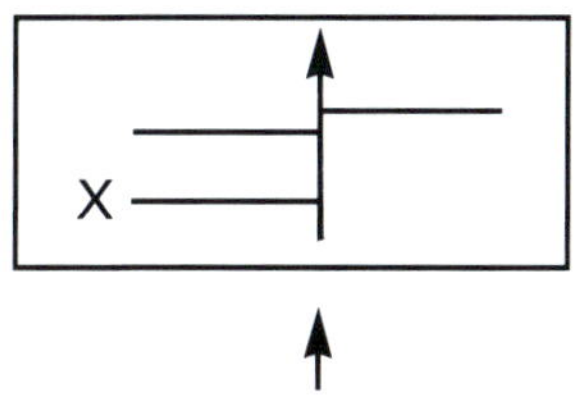

d.

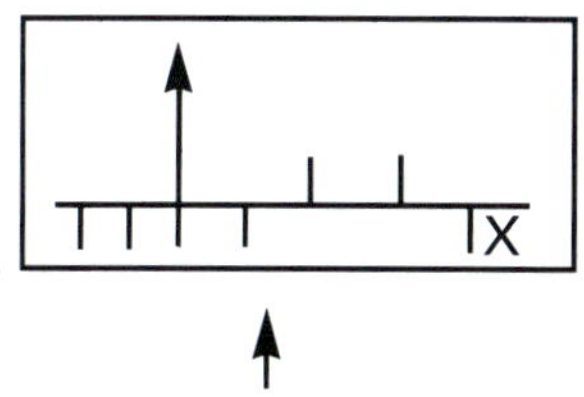

e.

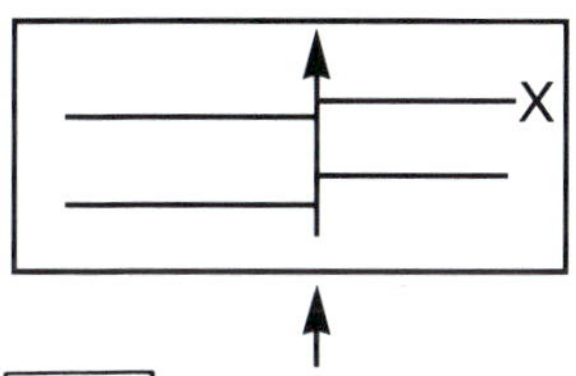

3 *Listen. Beatrix is at the Gare Centrale station in Brussels. She wants to go to the Teen Eye offices. She asks a policeman for help.*

Mark the route and the Teen Eye offices on the map.

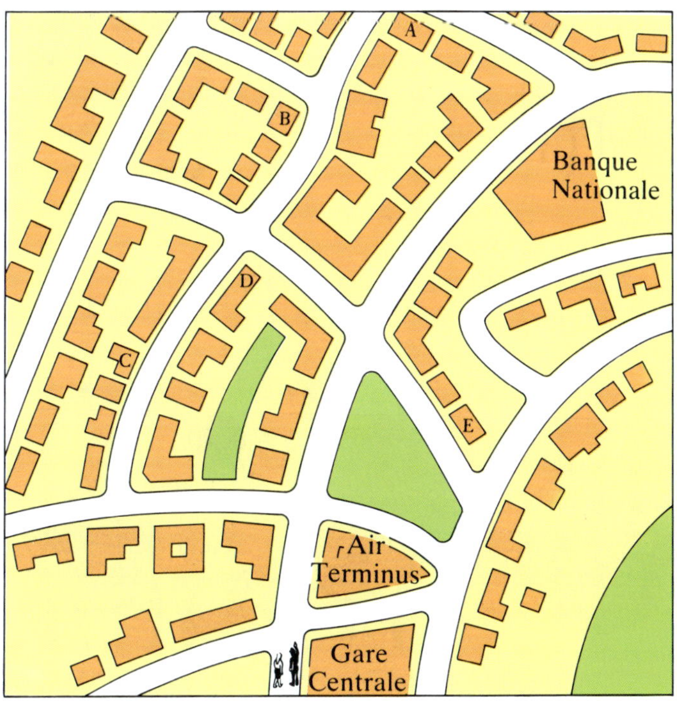

4 *Listen and repeat.*

How do I get to rue du Marais?
Go straight on.
Take the third turning on the left.
Turn first right.
It's the fourth building on the left.

5 *Look at the map. Work with your friend.*

a. Give each street a name.
b. Mark eight shops on the map.
c. Give each shop a street number.

6 *You are Beatrix and the policeman. Ask for directions to each of the shops.*

7 *Make a list of places near your school. Ask and answer how to get to these places from the school.*

► *eg* A: How do I get to the bus stop?
B: Go straight ahead. Take the first turning on the right, then the first on the left.

Unit 2c The Teen Eye programmes

Jane is talking to members of the Teen Eye team about how the programmes are made.

1 *Join the verbs and the information to make sentences.*

	☐ a. transmit	the programme.
	☐ b. choose	the script for the programme.
	☐ c. collect	subjects for each programme.
We	☐ d. write	films and photographs.
	☐ e. produce	the programme to the satellite.
	☐ f. go	the programme with members of the Teen Eye team.
	☐ g. discuss	to locations in Britain and abroad to get extra film and information.

2 *Listen and check your answers. Then listen again and number the sentences in the order you hear them.*

3 *Listen again. Put up your hand when you hear these words:*

first   and   then   and then   after that   next   so

4 *Number the pictures in the right order.*

5 *Read.*

We eat **and** sleep.
I wash my face **then** clean my teeth.
First I wash my face **and then** I clean my teeth.

He's cold **so** he's drinking a cup of hot coffee.

To make instant coffee, first he puts coffee powder into a cup **and then** he adds hot water. **Next** he puts milk and sugar into the coffee. **After that** he drinks it.

6 *Write the sentences in Exercise 1. Join them using these words:*

so   and   then   and then   next   after that   first

► *eg* We choose subjects for each programme **and then** we collect films and photographs.

7 *You and your partner are Jane and Pedro. Ask and answer about the programme. Use these questions.*

How do you organise the programmes?

What happens next?

Then what happens?

a. ☐

b. ☐

c. ☐

d. ☐

e. ☐

f. ☐

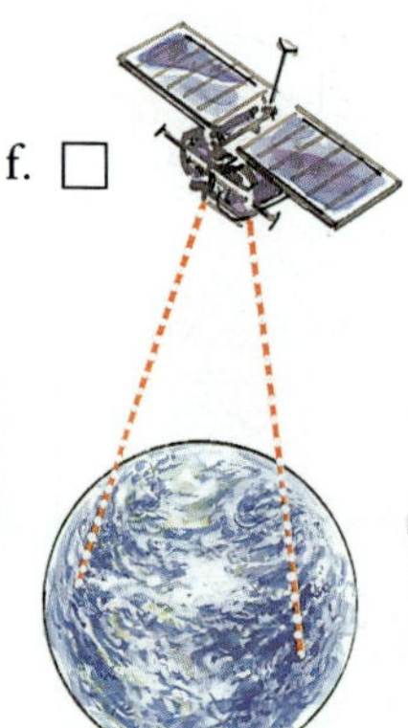

g. ☐

present simple tense p 105   /e/ next

Unit 2d Turn right at the post office

1 *Write the questions.*

A: ....?
B: My favourite sport is tennis.
A: ....?
B: I play in a park near my house.
A: ....?
B: It's easy. I go to the post office. Then I turn right and there's a little park on the right.
A: ....?
B: Of course! We can play together.

2 *Your pen-friend and his or her family are coming to your house for the first time. Write a short letter to the father of your pen-friend. Tell him how to get to your house from the station or bus stop. Draw him a little map.*

Unit 2 — Chatterbox A

Chatterbox B see page *93*.

1 *Look at the map. Write the name of these places, next to the* **even** *numbers (2, 4, 6 etc.). Then answer your friend's questions.*

football stadium   doctor's   bank   your house
park   record shop

2 *Ask your friend how to get to these places:*

police station   post office   his/her house
swimming pool   sports centre   supermarket

► *eg* A: Excuse me. How do I get to the police station?
B: Oh, that's easy. You . . .

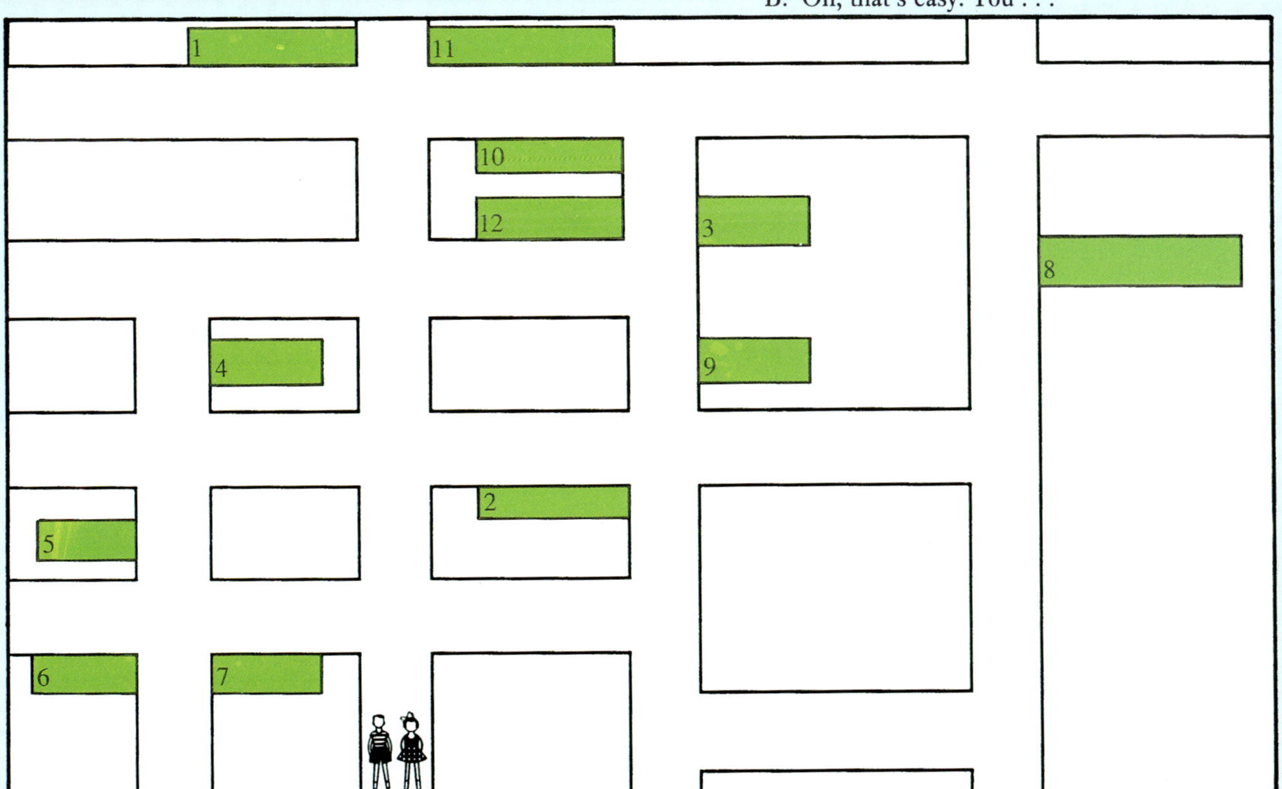

Unit 3a Do you ever go horse-riding?

1 *Write* **S** *(= sport) or* **OA** *(= other activity).*

...... play cards
...... go horse-riding
...... play basketball
...... drink coffee
...... do athletics
...... listen to the radio
...... go roller skating
...... play video games
...... go swimming
...... read English books

2 *Listen. Tick (√) or cross (×) Beatrix and Alan's sports.*

	horse-riding	swimming	roller skating	athletics
Beatrix				
Alan				

3 *Listen again. Write Alan, Annie or Beatrix under the pictures:*

a. ....

b. ....

c. ....

d. ....

4 *Listen and repeat.*

Do you ever go swimming?
Yes, I do./No, I don't.
Does she ever go horse-riding?
Yes, she does./No, she doesn't.
I don't know.

5 *Ask and answer about Beatrix and Alan. Use the activities in Exercise 2.*

► eg A: Does Beatrix ever go horse-riding?
B: Yes, she does.

6 *Ask and answer. Use the activities in Exercise 1.*

► *eg* A: Do you ever play cards?
B: Yes, I do./No, I don't.

7 *Now ask another friend about their partner.*

► *eg* A: Does Maria/Nick ever play cards?
C: Yes, she/he does./No, she/he doesn't.

Unit 3b How often do you play?

1 *Karin and Mikis are talking about the sports they do. Listen. Tick (√) the sports Mikis does and cross (×) the ones he doesn't do.*

a. ☐

b. ☐

c. ☐

d. ☐

2 *Listen again and join Karin's sports to the adverbs used.*

tennis swimming roller skating ice skating

sometimes usually often never

3 *Listen and repeat.*

How often do you play tennis?
I usually play twice a week in the summer.
Do you do the high jump?
No, never.

4 *Make a list of all the sports you know or do. Then ask and answer.*

▶ *eg* A: Do you ever play tennis?
B: Yes, I do.
A: How often do you play?
B: I usually play every afternoon in the summer.

5 *Fatma is asking Mikis what he does in his free time. Write the questions and practise the dialogue.*

Fatma: ....?
Mikis: The theatre? Yes, I sometimes go with my parents.
Fatma: ....?
Mikis: Oh, yes. I go with my friends. I like films.
Fatma: ....?
Mikis: Yes, I run and I do the high jump.
Fatma: ....?
Mikis: No, never, but I ride a bicycle!

6 *Answer these questions about yourself. Write complete sentences.*

What do you	never sometimes often usually always	do on Sundays?

adverbs of frequency p 107 /n/ **never**

Unit 3c Beatrix and her horse

a. ☐

b. ☐

c. ☐

d. ☐

e. ☐

f. ☐

1 *Beatrix is talking about her horse. Listen and number the pictures in the right order.*

2 *Listen again and answer these questions.*

a. Where does Trigger live?
b. When does Beatrix usually go and see him?
c. What does Beatrix do when she arrives at the stables?
d. Does she always go riding?
e. Where does she ride?
f. Does she ever ride alone?
g. What does she do near the lake?
h. Who eats Beatrix's picnic lunch?
i. How does Beatrix feel when she goes home?

3 *Listen again and tick (√) each time you hear these words.*

always ....
sometimes ....
often ....
usually ....
never ....

4 *Read and fill in the chart.*

Karin Jager lives in Copenhagen and her best friend, Greta, lives in Karstrup, a town near the capital. Karin and Greta often meet at the weekend and play sports together. In the winter they often go cycling and they sometimes go ice skating together. Cycling is very popular in Denmark and so is tennis and football. Karin and Greta never play football but they usually play tennis in the summer. In the spring they sometimes go sailing. There are no big rivers in Denmark but water sports are very popular on the lakes or in the sea.

season	sport	adverb
winter		
winter		
summer		
spring		

5 *Use the information in the chart and write sentences about Karin and Greta.*

Unit 3d Strange brothers

1 *Read. Then write the name of the brother under each picture.*

Gerry and Paul Sanders are identical twins but they are very different people. Gerry never drinks coffee and Paul never drinks tea. When Paul writes letters to me he sometimes writes back-to-front. I have to hold them in front of a mirror to read them. Gerry never writes back-to-front. Gerry always gets up late but he's never late for school. Paul usually gets up early but he's always late for school! Paul likes the cinema and he goes every Saturday with his friends. Gerry doesn't like films and never goes to the cinema. On Saturday when his brother goes to the cinema Gerry stays at home and does his homework. Paul never does his homework on Saturday. He always does it on Sunday afternoon.

a. ....

b. ....

c. ....

d. ....

e. ....

2 *Read again. Then ask and answer.*

▶ *eg* A: Does Gerry ever drink coffee?
B: No, he doesn't.

Unit 3 — *Chatterbox A*

Chatterbox B see page *94*.

1 *Ask your friend questions about Alan. Fill in the chart.*

▶ *eg* A: When does Alan go to the cinema?
B: He usually goes on Saturday but he sometimes goes on Sunday.

2 *Answer your friend's questions.*

	always	**usually**	**often**	**sometimes**	**never**
go to the cinema		on Saturday		on Sunday	
go to the beach					
play tennis		in the summer			in the winter
telephone friends			in the afternoon		in the morning
clean his teeth	in the morning		in the evening		
ride a bike					
go roller skating					
play volleyball		on Tuesday		on Thursday	
do homework					
read English books			at school	at home	
go to bed					

Unit 4a How much is it?

1 *Join the countries and units of money.*

Britain	mark
Germany	dollar
France	pound
Spain	franc
Italy	peseta
Japan	lira
America	yen
Greece	guilder
Holland	drachma

2 *Look at the English coins on page 121. Answer the questions.*

a. What is the smallest number of coins you need to make:

£3.00 £3.55 £4.26 £4.70 £1.80 £2.99

b. To express one and a half pounds, we say **one pound fifty** and we write **£1.50.**

Say these amounts:
£5.50 £4.25 £3.33 £12.93 £1.67 £8.34

3 *Alan is in a bicycle shop in Brussels. Listen and fill in the dialogue.*

4 *Listen again and tick (√)* ***True*** *or* ***False.***

	True	False
a. Alan wants to rent a bicycle.	☐	☐
b. The blue bicycle is expensive.	☐	☐
c. He rents a green bicycle.	☐	☐
d. He buys a pair of gloves.	☐	☐
e. He rides a bicycle a lot.	☐	☐

5 *Listen and repeat.*

How much is it?
It's 600 francs.
That's a bit expensive.
How much are they?
They're 280 francs.
They're quite cheap.

6 *Look at the pictures. Ask and answer.*

▶ *eg* A: How much is the book?
B: It's £3.99

present simple tense p 105, How much is it? /tʃ/ **cheap**

Unit 4b You must stop!

1 *Write the numbers from the picture in column 1.*

1	2	
☐	☐	Go round
☐	☐	Turn left
☐	☐	Don't ride bicycles
☐	☐	Go this way only

1	2	
☐	☐	Stop
☐	☐	Turn right
☐	☐	Don't enter
☐	☐	Don't carry big or heavy things

2 *Alan is in the bicycle hire shop. Listen and, in column 2, tick (√) the instructions you hear.*

3 *Listen and repeat.*

What does that sign mean?
It means you must stop.
What does it mean?
It means you mustn't ride bicycles here.

4 *Look at the picture again. Ask and answer.*

► *eg* A: Look at number 6. What's the problem?
B: You mustn't carry big or heavy things on a bicycle.
A: Look at number 3. What's the problem?
B: When you see this sign you must stop.

---

5 *Look at these signs outside the Zoo. Use the words and write sentences.*

a. ....  touch

b. ....  grass

c. ....  feed

d. ....  drop

e. ....  pick

f. ....  ride

Unit 4c I love my bike!

1 *Read the sentences. Then name the parts of the bicycle.*

a. You sit on a saddle.
b. Brakes stop a bike.
c. Tyres are round and full of air.
d. The bell is on the handlebars.
e. Lights are on at night.
f. You hold the handlebars.
g. The chain joins the pedals and the back wheel.
h. Your feet go on the pedals.

2 *Read the brochure about bicycles. Then match the parts of the bicycle and the instructions.*

3 *Write six sentences about keeping your bicycle safe.*

▶ *eg* You must check the handlebars every week.
You must see if they are straight.

4 *Find these words.*

bell
brakes
chain
deposit
gloves
hire
left
must
pedals
~~ride~~
right
saddle
stop
straight on
tyres
wheel

I G L O V E S O D K U
S C O U D B A J E L O
R T H I R E D K P O U
D E R A I L D O O I P
E A R A I L L A S R M
B R E A I N E C I K L
R R N C R G W G T E L
A T Y R E S H D F C A
K D M U S T E T K R E
E N U R A O E H O P A
S L A D E P L H E N L

KEEP YOUR BIKE SAFE
YOU MUST CHECK YOUR BICYCLE REGULARL

EVERY WEEK

CHECK

saddle
brakes
tyres
pedals
lights
handlebars
chain
bell

HOW

put a little oil on it
see if they are straight
turn them on and off
sit on bike and see if they are flat
ring it
move with them off and then put them on
sit and touch the ground with your feet
sit on the bike and put your feet on them

must, mustn't p 107 /b/ **b**ell

Unit 4d We must be quiet!

1 Listen and number the pictures.

a. ☐

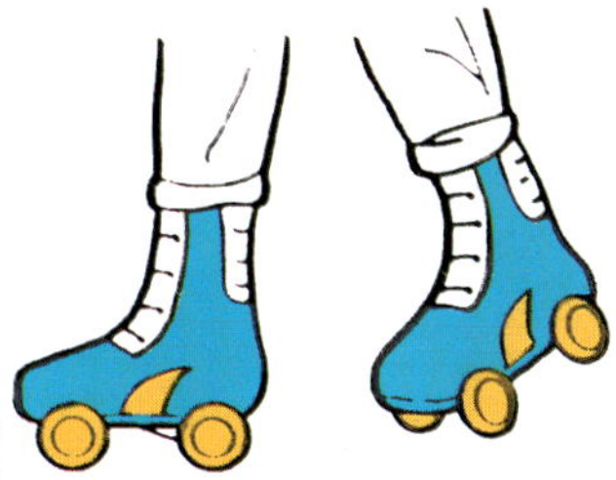
b. ☐

c. ☐

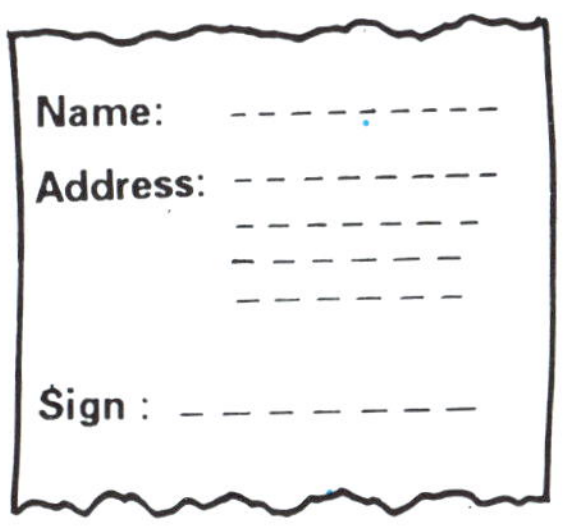

d. ☐

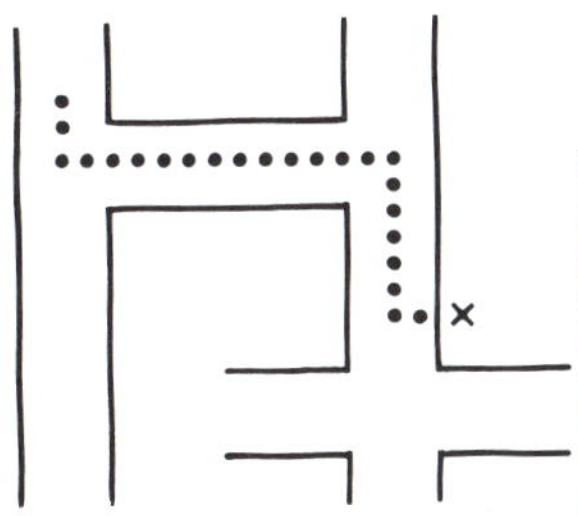
e. ☐

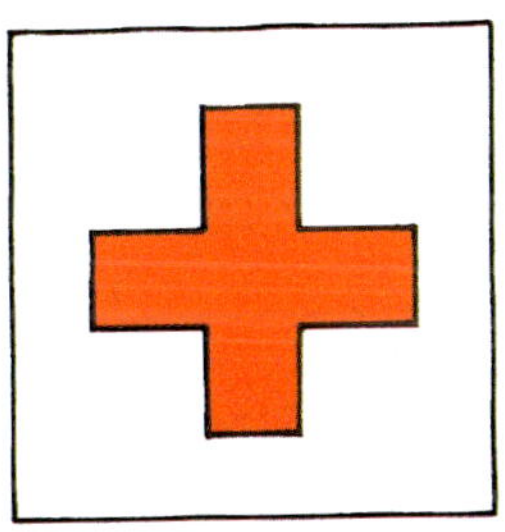
f. ☐

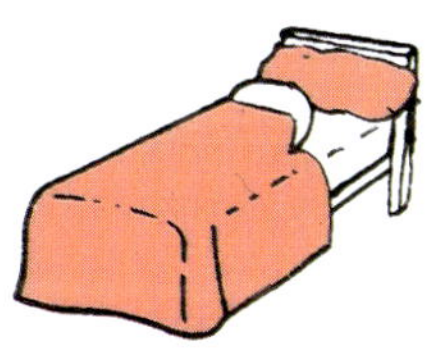
g. ☐

2 *Listen again. Tick (√)* ***True*** *or* ***False****.*
Correct the false statements.

	True	False
a. We must be quiet near the hospital.	☐	☐
b. The cinema is on your right.	☐	☐
c. Skating is on Wednesday morning.	☐	☐
d. You must go to bed early before an examination.	☐	☐
e. I must write your name and address.	☐	☐
f. You can leave your bicycle here.	☐	☐
g. The tennis competition is at the Youth Club.	☐	☐

Unit 4 Chatterbox A

Chatterbox B see page *94*.

1 *Read.*

once a day twice a week three times a month
four times a year

2 *Ask your friend questions about Mikis* (M) *and Jane* (J). *Fill in the chart.*

▶ *eg* A: How often does Mikis clean his teeth? (M2)
B: He cleans his teeth twice a day.
A: How often does Jane clean her teeth? (J3)
B. She cleans her teeth three times a day.

3 *Answer your friend's questions.*

Action	Day	Week	Month	Year
clean teeth	J3 M2			
go to the dentist				M3
play tennis			J3	
buy new records			M4	
play cards				J4
go swimming		M2		
have a party				J3
go to a party		J1		
wash hair		M1		
ride a bicycle				J2

Unit 5 Language check

Teen Eye on Pets

1 *Match the words and the pictures.*

1. bird 2. cat 3. dog 4. fish 5. hamster 6. lion
7. monkey 8. rabbit 9. snake 10. tortoise

2 *Read and answer in small groups.*

a. Have you got a pet? Have your friends got pets? Make a list.
b. Which animals are very popular? Which animals are not very popular?
c. What food does each pet eat?
d. Make a list of other animals you can have as pets. What foods do they eat?

3 *Look at the pictures. Describe one of the pictures. Your friend must guess which picture.*

a. ☐

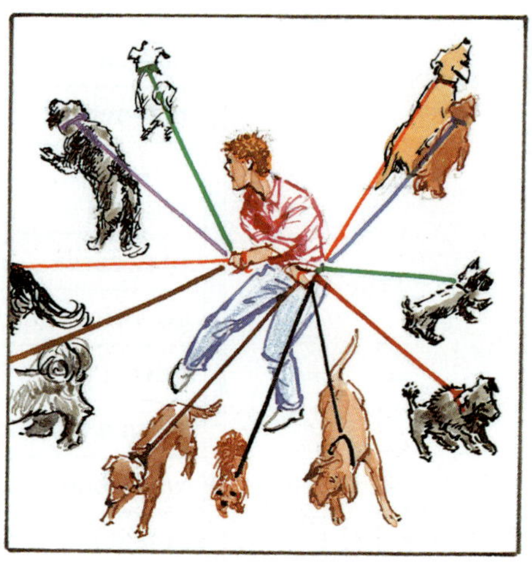

b. ☐

c. ☐

d. ☐

4 *Listen to Part One. Tick (√) the animals Linda Rose talks about.*

☐	dogs	☐	rabbits
☐	lions	☐	hamsters
☐	snakes	☐	tortoises
☐	birds	☐	cats

5 *Listen to Part Two. Number the animals in the order Andrew talks about them.*

☐ fish
☐ rabbits
☐ cats
☐ dogs
☐ birds
☐ hamsters

6 *Listen to Part Two again. Number the pictures in Exercise 3 in the right order.*

7 *Listen to Part Two again. Number the jobs in the order Andrew does them.*

☐ open the shop door carefully
☐ clean the bird cages
☐ open tins of cat and dog food
☐ feed all the other animals
☐ take the dogs for a walk
☐ brush the dogs
☐ wash the floors and clean the cages

8 *Write about Andrew's Saturday job. Use the sentences in Exercise 7.*

9 *Read the brochure from Swansea Zoo. Then fill in the missing questions and answers.*

a. Where do the elephants come from?
They ....
b. ....?
They come from India.
c. ....?
.... the Arctic.
d. ....?
.... Tanzania.
e. What .... the zoo ....?
It .... nine o'clock.
f. ....?
.... four o'clock.
g. .... zoo .... and close on ....?
It opens at ten o'clock and closes at three o'clock.
h. .... much .... the ....?
For adults they are £1.20.
i. .... much .... for ....
12 years old?
They are 80p.
j. .... mustn't .... do in the zoo?
You .... touch ....
k. .... do?
You .... clean.

Visit Swansea Zoo!

Come and see the African elephants and the new tigers from India. The Arctic bears are waiting to meet you, and the monkeys from Zaire are waiting to throw things at you. The hyenas from Tanzania are waiting to laugh at you, and the giraffes from Zambia are waiting to look down on you.

Tickets

Adults: £1.20
Children: Over 12: 80p
Under 12: Free

Opening times

9.00 – 4.00
except Fridays
10.00 – 3.00

SCHOOL PARTIES WELCOME

KEEP THE ZOO CLEAN

DO NOT
FEED, TOUCH, OR GO NEAR
THE ANIMALS

Unit 6a What are you doing tonight?

Alan is talking to his sister, Sarah.

1 *Listen and answer these questions.*

a. What's Alan doing tonight?
b. What's he doing next Wednesday?
c. How long is he speaking for?
d. Why does Sarah say 'How awful!'?

2 *Listen and repeat.*

What are you doing tonight?
I'm watching a programme on television.
How long are you speaking for?
I'm speaking for about ten minutes.

3 *Ask and answer from this table. Write the answers.*

► *eg* A: What are you doing tonight?
B: I'm watching television.

What	are	you	doing	tonight? tomorrow afternoon? next weekend? next summer? next Christmas?
Where	is	she he	going	

4 *Ask another friend about his or her partner.*

► *eg* A: What is she doing tonight?
B: She's watching television.

5 *Read and practise this dialogue. Then make other dialogues.*

Alan: Are you going to the Youth Club tonight?
Susan: To the Youth Club? What's happening there?
Alan: We are playing the Oxford table tennis team.
Susan: Oh, great! I'm definitely watching that!

a. Youth Club/tonight
play/Oxford table tennis
watch

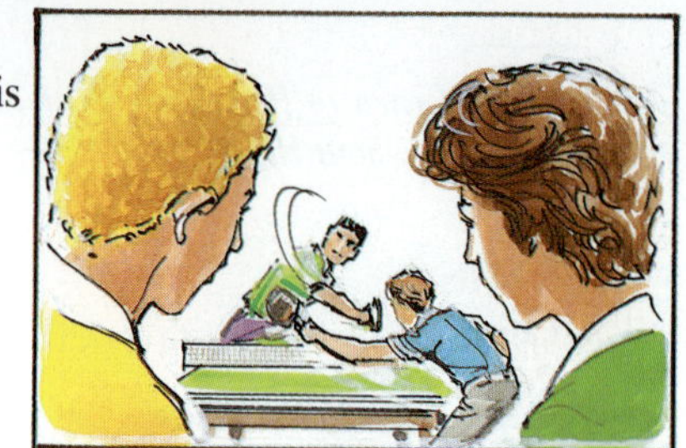

b. Sports Club/next Friday
play/Cardiff football
watch

c. Cricket Club/tomorrow afternoon have/party
go to

d. Sports Club/tomorrow
plan/darts match
enter

e. disco/next Saturday
have/fancy dress party
go to

6 *Write one of the dialogues.*

present continuous tense (as future) p 106 /ŋ/ doing

Unit 6b How well can you swim?

1 *Tick (√) how well you can do these things.*

	not at all	well	badly	very well
swim				
roller skate				
play tennis				
speak English				
play chess				
speak French				
ride a horse				

2 *Listen to how well Mikis and Karin can do some sports. In the chart write M (= Mikis) or K (= Karin).*

3 *Listen and repeat.*

Can you swim?
Yes, I can.
How well can you swim?
I can swim very well.

4 *Ask and answer. Use the ideas in Exercise 1.*

► *eg* A: Can you swim?
B: Yes, I can.
A: How well can you swim?
B: I can swim very well.

5 *Match the verbs and the pictures. Then ask a friend how well he or she can do these things.*

knit sing act play guitar

a. ....

b. ....

c. ....

d. ....

6 *Write about your friend. Say how well he or she can do the things in Exercise 5.*

verb *can* (ability) p 105, adverbs of ability p 107 /iː/ speak /ɪ/ swim

Unit 6c How long are you staying?

1 *Make a list of at least seven different ways of travelling. Then answer the questions.*

a. Which way do you usually travel?
b. Which is your favourite way of travelling?
c. Why?
d. Which way don't you like?
e. Why?

2 *Beatrix is asking Alan about his next Christmas holidays. Listen to Part One and tick (√)* ***True*** *or* ***False****. Correct the false statements.*

	True	False
a. Alan's going to Sardinia at Christmas.	☐	☐
b. He's staying with his uncle Antonio.	☐	☐
c. He's staying for two weeks.	☐	☐

3 *Listen and repeat.*

Where are you going next Christmas?
I'm going to Sardinia.
Who are you staying with?
I'm staying with Antonio.

4 *Listen to Part Two and number the places in the order you hear them.*

☐ Olbia
☐ London
☐ Milan airport
[1] Sardinia
☐ Cardiff
☐ Milan station
☐ Genoa

5 *Listen again. Write where and how Alan is travelling.*

6 *Write sentences. Use the information in Exercise 5.*

► *eg* He's travelling from Cardiff to London by car.

7 *Ask a friend about his or her plans for:*

this evening   tomorrow morning   next weekend
next Christmas

► *eg* A: What are you doing this evening?
B: I'm going to my friend's house.

8 *Ask another friend about his or her partner.*

► *eg* A: What's he doing this evening?
B: He's going to his friend's house.

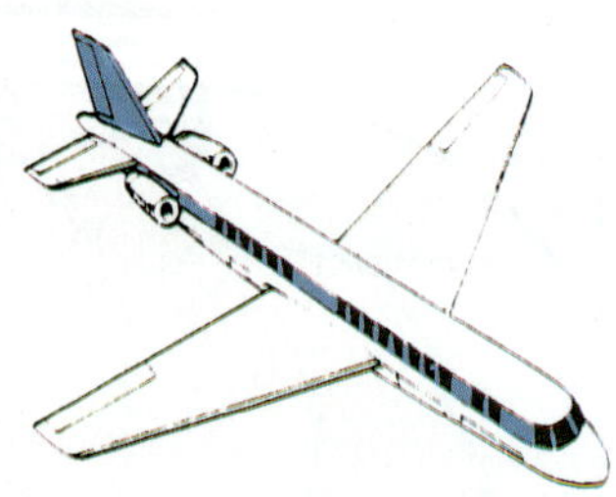

From: Cardiff	From:	From:	From:	From: ....
To:	To:	To:	To:	To: ....
By:	By:	By:	By:	By: ....

present continuous tense (as future) p 106   /w/ **wh**ich

Unit 6d Pedro's holiday

Pedro had a holiday in France with Françoise and her family.

Unit 6 *Chatterbox A*

Chatterbox B see page *95*.

1 Ask your friend questions about what Pedro and Françoise did. Fill in the chart.

► *eg* A: What did Pedro do on Sunday morning?
B: He arrived in Rouen.

2 *Answer your friend's questions.*

	Morning	Afternoon	Evening
Sunday 21	Pedro arrived in Rouen	They	They had dinner in a restaurant
Monday 22	They	They	Pedro wrote some postcards
Tuesday 23	They walked into the town	They	They went to the Youth Club and met a lot of friends
Wednesday 24	They	They walked around Paris and looked at the monuments	They
Thursday 25	Françoise and Pedro left Rouen to go to Paris airport	Pedro	Pedro flew back to Lisbon

Read Pedro's postcard to Jane. Then write the postcard he sent to Derek on Wednesday evening.

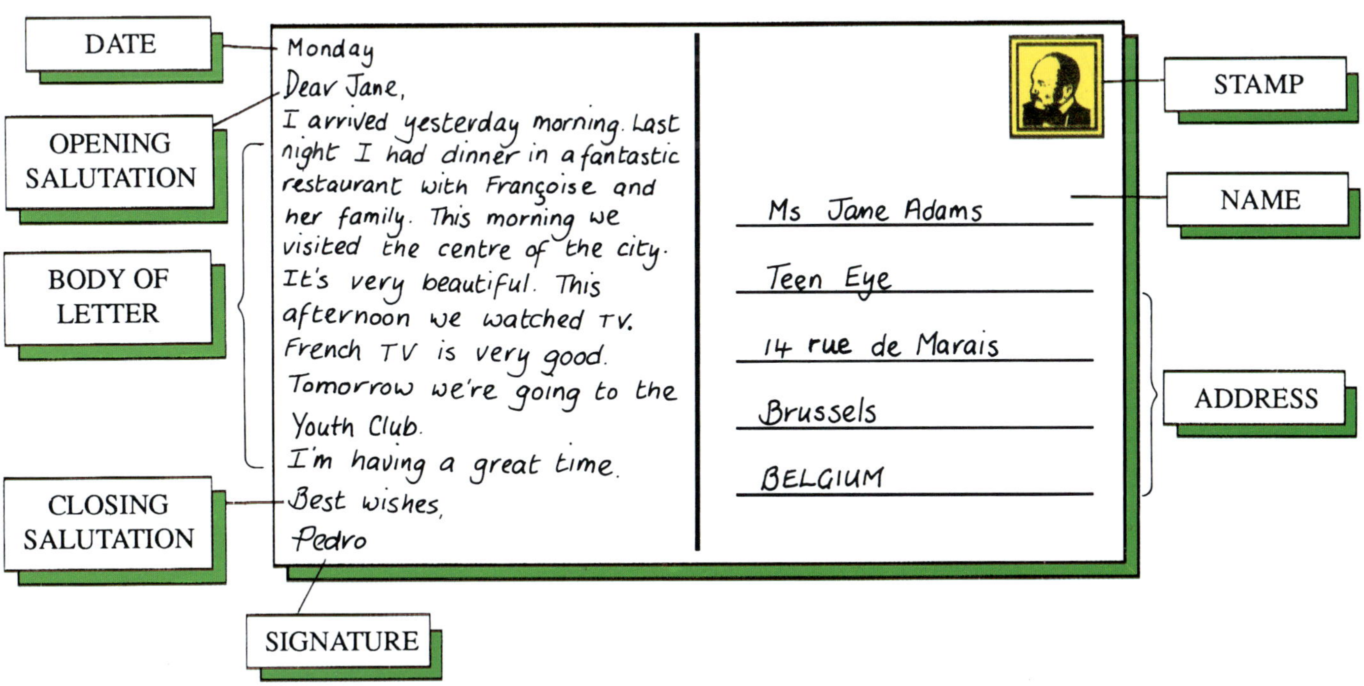

past simple tense p 106 /ɪd/ visit**ed** /d/ arriv**ed** /t/ watch**ed**

Unit 7a Did you have a good time?

1 *Match the animals, the sounds they make and the verbs.*

a. b. c. d.

Woof woof!	☐	It crows.	☐
Cock-a-doodle-doo!	☐	It cheeps.	☐
Miaow!	☐	It barks.	☐
Tweet tweet!	☐	It mews.	☐

2 *Jane Adams is talking to Derek. Listen and tick (√)* ***True*** *or* ***False****. Correct the false statements.*

	True	False
a. Derek stayed with his aunt last weekend.	☐	☐
b. He went to the seaside.	☐	☐
c. He went to the country last month.	☐	☐
d. He stayed with his aunt for one week.	☐	☐
e. He got up at five o'clock every morning.	☐	☐

3 *Listen and repeat.*

Where did you go last weekend?
I went to the country.
Where did you stay?
I stayed with my aunt.
Did you have a good time?
Yes, I did.

4 *Ask a friend questions about the sentences in Exercise 2. Start with these words:*

a. Who? b. Where? c. When? d. How long?
e. What time?

► *eg* A: Who did Derek stay with?
B: He stayed with his aunt.

5 *Write the missing words. Then practise the dialogue.*

Derek: Where .... for your last half-term holiday?
Pedro: I went to France.
Derek: What .... there?
Pedro: I visited Françoise. Do you remember her?
Derek: I certainly do. She lives in Rouen, doesn't she?
Pedro: Yes, that's right.
Derek: How ....?
Pedro: I flew to Paris and then got a train to Rouen.
Derek: How long ....?
Pedro: Oh, about five days. I returned to Lisbon on the 25th.
Derek: Did .... time?
Pedro: Yes, we had a fantastic time. We really enjoyed ourselves.

6 *Write a dialogue, between you and your teacher, about your last holiday.*

past simple tense p 106, WH questions p 108 /ɔː/ dawn /ɒ/ cl

Unit 7b You speak French, don't you?

1 *Listen and read. Then tick (√) **True** or **False**.*

Mikis: Teen Eye. Can I help you? *Einen augenblick, bitte.* Karin, can Jane speak German?
Karin: I think so but I'm not sure.
Mikis: Ask her. There's a call from Germany.
Karin: Jane! You can speak German, can't you?
Jane: Yes, I can. Why?
Karin: There's a phone call from Germany in the office.
Jane: Oh, good. I'm coming.

	True	False
a. Karin is certain Jane can speak German.	☐	☐
b. Karin thinks Jane can speak German, but she isn't certain.	☐	☐
c. Karin doesn't think Jane can speak German.	☐	☐

2 *Listen and read. Then tick (√) **True** or **False**.*

Fatma likes coffee ice-cream, doesn't she?
Yes, I think so.

	True	False
a. Mikis thinks Fatma likes coffee ice-cream, but he's not sure.	☐	☐
b. Mikis is certain Fatma likes coffee ice-cream.	☐	☐
c. Mikis doesn't think Fatma likes coffee ice-cream.	☐	☐

3 *Read.*

Mikis **is** busy, **isn't** he?
Alan and Sarah **are** Welsh, **aren't** they?
Jane **speaks** German, **doesn't** she?
Jane and Derek **speak** French, **don't** they?

4 *Match the sentences and the question tags.*

a. Our teacher comes from England,	isn't he?
b. You're French,	wasn't he?
c. You study English,	doesn't he/she?
d. Your friend's a very tall boy,	can't they?
e. Our teacher wakes up early,	don't you?
f. You were in Spain last year,	doesn't he/she?
g. He was good at English last term,	aren't you?
h. They can swim well,	weren't you?

5 *Listen and repeat the answers to Exercise 4.*

6 *Ask and answer. Use the sentences in Exercise 4.*

► *eg* A: Our teacher comes from England, doesn't he/she?
B: Yes, he/she does./No, he/she doesn't./I think so.

Unit 7c He's going to score a goal!

1 *Match the words and the people in the picture.*

☐ catch ☐ fall down ☐ fall off ☐ jump over ☐ score ☐ throw
☐ dive ☐ fall into ☐ hit ☐ kick ☐ swim into

2 *Look at the pictures. Ask and answer.*

► *eg* A: Look at that boy. What's he going to do?
B: He's going to kick the ball.

3 *Write about each picture. Say what is going to happen.*

4 *Answer the questions.*

a. When is your next birthday?
b. How old are you going to be?
c. What are you going to do on your birthday?

5 *Alan wants a birthday party. Listen and answer the questions.*

a. When is Alan going to have his party?
....
b. How many friends is Sarah going to invite?
....
c. Is she happy about this?
....
d. What are they going to eat at the party?
....
e. What are they going to drink?
....
f. What are they going to do at the party?
....
g. Who is Alan going to invite?
....

6 *Write the dialogue between Alan, his mother and Sarah. Use your answers to Exercise 5 to help you.*

future form: *going to* p 106 /g/ **g**oal /k/ **c**oal

Unit 7d A day out

Unit 7 *Chatterbox A*

Chatterbox B see page *96*.

1 *Read the story and start to fill in the chart.*

2 *Ask your friend questions and complete the chart.*

► *eg* A: When are they going?
Where are they going in the afternoon?
What time are they going to arrive in Swansea?

3 *Answer your friend's questions.*

Next Saturday the Bailey family – mother, father, Alan and his sister Sarah – are going to drive to Swansea for the day. They are going to get up at six o'clock and they are going to leave home at 7.30, after breakfast. In Swansea they are going to visit the Glynn Vivian Art Gallery when it opens at 9.30. The gallery has some beautiful pottery and paintings. At twelve o'clock they are all going to the beach. They are going to swim in the sea and then Alan's father is going to buy some sandwiches for lunch.

In the afternoon, Sarah and her father are going to go fishing in the sea in a small boat. Fishing is very popular in Swansea, but if they do not catch any fish, they are going to buy some fish for dinner at home.

All the family are going to meet and have tea together and then drive home to Cardiff for dinner.

Family's surname:	....	Time/get up?	....	**Afternoon**	
First names:		What/breakfast?	....	Father and daughter:	
Father	....	Time/leave home?	....	Where/go?	....
Mother	....	Time/arrive Swansea?	....	What/do?	....
Son	....			Mother and son:	
Daughter	....	**Morning**		Where/go?	....
		Where/visit?	....	Who/visit?	....
Date of trip	....	What/do then?	....	What/take?	....
Day of trip	....	Time/go/beach?	....	Family:	
Where/trip to?	....	What/do/beach?	....	Where/meet?	....
How/travel?	....	Who/buy/sandwiches?	....	Time/meet?	....
How long/journey?	....	Where/lunch?	....	What/dinner?	....

On Monday, Alan's teacher asked the class to write about the weekend. You are Alan. Write about your visit to Swansea. Try to use these past tense verbs:

bought (buy) caught (catch) drove (drive) got up (get up)
had (have) left (leave) met (meet) swam (swim)
took (take) went (go)

Unit 8a Why don't we go to France?

1 *Number these activities in the order you like them (1–6).*

☐ go/cinema	☐ visit/museums
☐ go/theatre	☐ play/tennis
☐ watch/football match	☐ go/shopping

a. ☐ b. ☐ c. ☐

2 *Jane is talking to Fatma. Look at the pictures and put them in the right order.*

3 *Listen and check your answers for Exercise 2. Then answer the questions.*

a. Jane makes two suggestions. What are they?
b. Does Fatma agree to them?

4 *Listen and repeat.*

Why don't we go to France next week?
That's a good idea.
What about going to Paris?
I'd love to but I can't.

5 *Ask and answer. Use the places in Exercise 1.*

▶ *eg* A: What about going to the cinema tonight?
B: That's a good idea.
A: Why don't we go to the cinema tomorrow?
B: I'd love to but I can't.

6 *Fill in the diary, but leave one day free. Then, in groups of five, ask and answer.*

▶ *eg* A: Why don't we go to the cinema on Saturday?
B: I'd love to but I can't. I'm playing volleyball on Saturday.

present simple tense p 105

/aɪ/ why /əʊ/ bow

Unit 8b How far is it from here?

1 *Jane and Fatma are at Charles de Gaulle airport near Paris. They want to go to Rouen. Listen and fill in the chart.*

From/To	Distance	Time by car
Paris–Rouen		

2 *Listen and repeat.*

How far is Rouen from here?
About a hundred and sixty kilometres.
How long does it take by car?
By car it takes about two hours.

3 *Read. Then answer the questions.*

Did you know . . .?

The first man to sail around the world alone was an American, Captain Joshua Slocum. In his yacht *Spray* he sailed 74,000 km. It took him 3 years, 3 months and ten days, from 24th April 1895 to 3rd July 1898. Captain Slocum was very brave because he couldn't swim!

a. Why is Captain Slocum famous?
b. What was the name of his yacht?
c. How long did it take him to sail around the world?

A man in Australia wanted to ride around the country on a horse. Henry G Perry took 157 days to ride the 22,565 km around Australia. He needed six horses!

a. How far is it around Australia?
b. How did Henry G Perry travel?
c. How long did the journey take?

In 1994 the Channel Tunnel opened between Folkestone and Calais. The train takes 35 minutes from platform to platform. The journey on this 300 kilometre-an-hour Eurostar train from London to Paris and Brussels through the tunnel takes 3 hours and 3 hours 15 minutes respectively.

a. When was the Channel Tunnel opened?
b. How long does it take to cross the Channel?
c. How long does it take from London to Brussels?
d. How fast does the Eurostar train go?

On 19th August 1988 a group of young people left London in a taxi. They travelled through 14 countries to Australia. The taxi arrived on 27th October 1988, 70 days later. The taxi fare for 22,000 km was £31,446!

a. Where did the taxi start the journey?
b. Where did it go to?
c. How much did the journey cost?

4 *Ask and answer. Use the information in Exercise 3.*

► *eg* A: How far did Henry Perry ride?
B: He rode 22,565 kilometres.
A: How long did it take him?
B: It took him 157 days.

5 *Find out the distances and travel times between places in your town or area. Then ask and answer.*

► *eg* A: How far is it from the town centre to the museum?
B: About three kilometres.
A: How long does it take by bus/car?
B: It takes about 20 minutes by bus/10 minutes by car.

Unit 8c Do you think they play tennis?

1 *Derek and Jane are talking about sports in different countries. Listen and tick (√) the answers.*

a. Where is basketball popular?

Germany ☐ Sweden ☐ Denmark ☐

b. Does Jane think basketball is popular in Italy?

Yes ☐ No ☐ Doesn't know ☐

c. Does Derek think ice skating is popular in hot countries?

Yes ☐ No ☐ Doesn't know ☐

2 *Listen again. Answer the questions.*

a. What is Derek's first question?
b. What is Jane going to do?
c. What is Derek going to do?

3 *Listen and repeat.*

Do you think they ice skate in hot countries?
It's possible.
Maybe.
I don't know.
Yes, they do.
No, they don't.

4 *Look at these sentences. Ask and answer.*

► *eg* A: Do you think Paris is a very expensive city?
B: Yes, I do./No, I don't./Maybe./It's possible.

Paris is a very expensive city.
Fatma works very hard.
Elephants eat a lot of fruit.
There are 400 million telephones in the world.
You can buy clothes in an English supermarket.
The Portuguese eat a lot of fish.

5 *Find out how many students think/don't think these statements are true.*

a. A person can run over 100 kilometres an hour.
b. A dog can run over 100 kilometres an hour.
c. An animal can run over 100 kilometres an hour.
d. A bird can fly over 100 kilometres an hour.
e. A fly can fly over 100 kilometres an hour.
f. A plane can fly over 100 kilometres an hour.
g. A person can hit a tennis ball over 100 kilometres an hour.

6 *Follow these instructions and make a questionnaire for Jane.*

a. In small groups, make a list of twelve sports.
b. Talk about the sports with the class. Agree a final list of twelve sports.

Follow the rest of the instructions on your own.

c. Divide a page into fifteen vertical columns.
d. Draw thirteen horizontal lines. Your page now has 195 boxes.
e. Write the vertical column headings at the top of the page: In column 1 write the word SPORTS. In columns 2–15 write the countries of the European Community and America and Argentina.
f. In the horizontal column headings down the side of the page, write the list of twelve sports that the class agreed.
g. Do a survey in the class, with another class or with the school. Each student must ask one other student each question. The question you must ask is:

Do you think that young people in ....? (*eg* France play tennis?)

If the answer is **Yes**, write a tick (√).
If the answer is **No**, write a cross (×).

7 *In groups of ten, make statistics like this:*

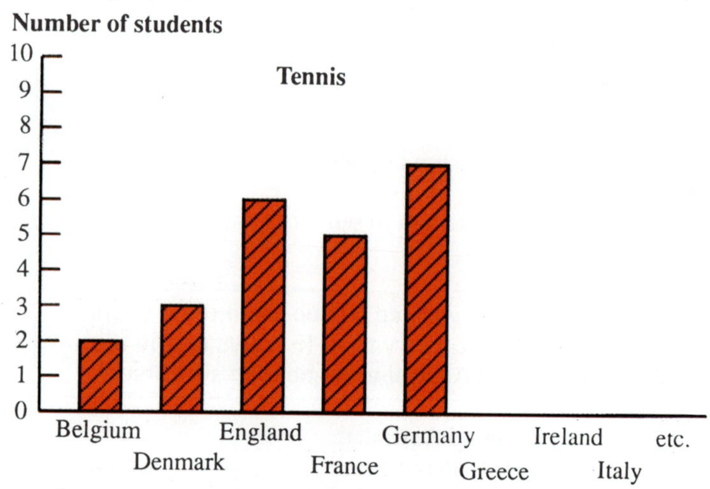

8 *Join your statistics together to make a class chart.*

imperatives p 107 /u:/ do

Unit 8d Dear Teacher

1 *This is the letter Derek sent to schools with Jane's questionnaire. Join the headings to the different parts of the letter. Then put the text of the letter in the right order.*

Headings

- date
- letterhead
- signature
- introduction
- opening salutation
- body of letter
- closing salutation
- conclusion

Text of the letter

a. **TEEN EYE**
14 rue du Marais
Brussels

b. 14 May, 19--

c. Dear Teacher,

d. Thanking you in anticipation of your help.
Yours faithfully,

e. *Derek Farley*
Derek Farley
Programme Director

f. **Teen Eye** is a satellite programme for Secondary school children. We produce programmes of interest to children throughout the world.

g. I am enclosing a questionnaire and would be very grateful if you would ask your class to fill it in and return it to us here in Brussels.

h. We would like to carry out a survey to find out which sports are played by children in different countries.

2 *Write a letter to a pen-friend club and ask for the names and addresses of some people of your age. Use the headings in Exercise 1 as a model.*

3 *Write a letter to a school friend asking about his/her hobbies and interests.*

4 *Exchange letters and write a reply. Remember to set out your letter using the headings in Exercise 1.*

Unit 8 Chatterbox A

Chatterbox B see page 97.

1 *Ask your friend questions. Fill in the chart.*

eg A: How far is the beach from the Teen Eye offices?
B: It's 120 kilometres.
A: How long does it take by car?
B: By car it takes 2 hours.

2 *Answer your friend's questions.*

Place	Distance	Car	Bicycle	Foot
the beach	120 km	2 hours	6 hours	
the cinema	2 km		15 minutes	
the lake		25 minutes		2 hours
the bus stop	650 m		2 minutes	
the station		8 minutes		20 minutes

Unit 9a Would you like to go there?

Jane is visiting Beatrix in Amsterdam.

1 *What do you know about the Netherlands? Read these sentences and tick (√) **True** or **False**.*

	True	False
a. There are a lot of canals in the Netherlands.	☐	☐
b. The Netherlands is in the south of Europe.	☐	☐
c. The Netherlands is famous for daffodils.	☐	☐
d. The Netherlands is famous for tulips.	☐	☐
e. The capital of the Netherlands is Amsterdam.	☐	☐
f. The people of the Netherlands are called Dutch.	☐	☐
g. The Netherlands is an island.	☐	☐

2 *Look at the map and find these places.*

Vincent van Gogh Museum
Old Church
Flower market
Anne Frank's house
Mint Tower
Vondel Park
Dam Square
Indonesian restaurants
Magere Bridge

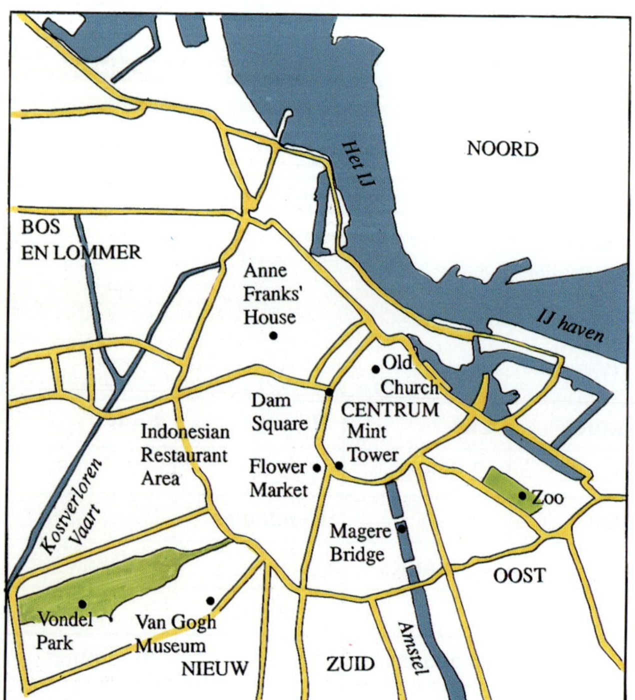

3 *Read the Guide to Amsterdam. Tick (√) the places in Exercise 2 that are in the Guide.*

Many people think Amsterdam is the capital of the Netherlands, but, in fact, The Hague is. Amsterdam is very popular with tourists because it is a beautiful city and there are many things to see and do.

Start your day with a boat trip and see the canals, or visit the flower market. There are two important museums in the city: the Rijksmuseum and the world famous Vincent van Gogh Museum. Anne Frank's house is a museum too. The main square is called Dam Square and lots of people meet there or in Vondel Park. Why not finish the evening with a meal in one of the many Indonesian restaurants?

4 *Listen. Which places in Exercise 2 are Jane and Beatrix going to visit?*

5 *Listen and repeat.*

Would you like to go to the Van Gogh Museum?
I'd love to.
Would you like to visit the flower market?
I don't think there's enough time this morning.

6 *Invite Jane to all the places in Exercise 2.*

► *eg* A: Would you like to go to the Vincent van Gogh Museum?
B: I'd love to./I don't think there's enough time today.

7 *Write down five interesting places in your town or area. Then invite your friends to visit them.*

would for invitations p 108   /f/ flower /v/ visit

Unit 9b Do you want to play tennis?

1 *Write* **play** *or* **go** *and the name of the activity for each picture.*

▶ *eg* a. play chess

a. ....

b. ....

c. ....

d. ....

e. ....

f. ....

g. ....

h. ....

2 *The Teen Eye team are organising a game of tennis. Listen and write who in the Teen Eye team asks and answers the questions.*

	Asks	Answers
a. Do you want to play tennis after lunch?	....	....
b. Do you want to play tennis this afternoon?	....	....
c. Would you like to play tennis this afternoon?	....	....

3 *Why is question c. different?*

4 *Listen and repeat.*

Do you want to play tennis this afternoon?
I'd love to but I can't. I must study.
Would you like to play tennis this afternoon?
Yes, I'd love to.

5 *Ask and answer. Use the activities in Exercise 1.*

▶ *eg* A: Do you want to play chess this afternoon?
B: Yes, I'd love to.
A: Do you want to go jogging this evening?
B: I'd love to but I can't. I must do my homework.

6 *Look at the pictures. With a friend write a dialogue between Beatrix, Mikis, Alfonso and Jane. Then, in groups of four, practise the dialogues.*

Unit 9c I'm afraid I can't come

Beatrix is having a party.

1 *Look at these sentences. Tick (√) **Good** or **Bad** reasons for not going to the party.*

	Good	Bad
a. I am ill.	☐	☐
b. My mother is ill.	☐	☐
c. My aunt is going to visit us.	☐	☐
d. I'm going to wash my hair.	☐	☐
e. I'm going to watch television.	☐	☐
f. I'm going out with my family.	☐	☐
g. I've got a music lesson.	☐	☐

A PARTY!

on Saturday September 17

at 15 Minervalaan, Nieuw Zuid, Amsterdam

time 5.30

from Beatrix van Dunn

to Jane Adams

RSVP

PLEASE COME IN JEANS!

2 *Read the invitation and Jane's letter. Answer the questions.*

a. Whose party is it?
b. Where is it?
c. What time is it?
d. What must you wear?
e. What does RSVP mean?
f. Where is Jane now?
g. When did she write the letter?
h. Who is the letter to?
i. Can Jane go to the party?
j. Why?
k. What does Jane hope?
l. How does she finish her letter?

3 *Listen and fill in Derek's letter.*

14 Rue du Marais
Brussels
Belgium

5th September

Dear Beatrix,

Thank you ________ your invitation.
I am ________ ________ that weekend and so
I ________ ________ to come to your party.
I am sure it ________ ________ ________
________ a ________ good ________ .
I am ________ forward to it and to ________
your ________ .
With ________ wishes,

Derek

14 Rue du Marais
Brussels
Belgium

3rd September

Dear Beatrix,
Thank you very much for the invitation to your party on 17th September.
I would love to come, but I'm afraid I can't.
I'm going to Scotland that weekend.
I hope you and your friends have a lovely time.

With best wishes,

Jane

4 *With a friend, write two letters to Beatrix. In one letter say you can go to her party. In the other letter say you can't go.*

past simple tense p 106 /tʃ/ watch /ʃ/ wash

Unit 9d Jane's party

1 *Listen to Jane's story about a birthday party. Number the pictures in the right order.*

a. ☐

b. ☐

c. ☐

d. ☐

e. ☐

f. ☐

3 *Look at the pictures in Exercise 1 and write the story. Try to use these words:*

and then and then after that

2 *Listen again. Fill in Jane's invitation to Michael.*

A PARTY!

on ....
at 34, ...
time ....
from ....
to ....

PLEASE COME IN JEANS!

Unit 9 Chatterbox A

Chatterbox B see page *97*.

1 *Ask your friend for the missing sentences in the dialogues. You may need to ask questions.*

► *eg* Can you repeat that, please?
How do you spell 'area', please?

2 *Dictate your sentences to your friend. Say the words in groups.*

► *eg* Do you want/
to come to my house/
this afternoon?

Dialogue 1

A: Do you want/to come to my house/this afternoon?
B: ....
A: I live in the north/of the town./ Here's my address.
B: ....
A: What time/are you going to come?
B: ....
A: Yes, that's fine./ Bring your football with you.
B: ....
A: Yes./ See you at four.
B: ....

Dialogue 2

A: ....
B: About three kilometres.
A: ....
B: It takes me/about five minutes.
A: ....
B: I come by car/with my father./ Do you come/by car?
A: ....
B: Do you live/near the school?
A: ....
B: Let's meet tomorrow/at your house/and come to school/together.

Unit 10 Language check

Teen Eye on the Highlands

1 *Choose what you think are the correct answers about Scotland. Then read the text and check your answers.*

a. The Scottish Highlands are an area of
A mountain scenery. **B** beaches. **C** hotels.

b. A loch is
A a river. **B** a lake. **C** an area of open land.

c. A kilt is
A a piece of clothing. **B** a gun. **C** a drink.

d. A clan is
A a container for cola. **B** a group of people. **C** a drink.

2 *Describe one of the pictures. Ask a friend to guess which one.*

3 *Read about the Highlands in Scotland then match the pictures and the paragraphs.*

1. The Scottish Highlands are an area in the north of Scotland where you can see wonderful mountain scenery. As well as mountains there are green valleys, hidden lochs and isolated villages which make the Highlands one of Europe's last true wildernesses.
2. Today Scotland is famous for whisky, tartan kilts, biscuits made with butter (called shortbread) and of course, Rob Roy. However, it is not commonly known that Scotland's history goes back a long way to the times of the Picts, Celts, and Vikings who settled there long before the Scottish clans, such as the McDonalds, the McGregors and the Camerons, that we know today.
3. A new tourist attraction that cost £1.2 million opened in 1995 to show this history. Highland Mysteryworld is built on a peninsula at Glencoe near Fort William. Actors and special effects dramatise the Highlands and their legends as they appeared to the ancient inhabitants.
4. The most famous of these legends is about the Seal Woman. This wild creature, half-seal, half-woman, kidnapped people and took them to her underwater home where she then killed them. Even today it is still possible to see the seals which swim in the loch at Fort William. Who knows – perhaps one of them is the Seal Woman coming back to find more people to kidnap!
5. The ancient Highlanders buried their dead with mysterious rituals. Prehistoric stone circles and burial areas can be found all over the region. One of the easiest sites to find is Clava Cairns near Inverness. It has three large burial chambers surrounded by tall stones and dates from about 2000 BC.
6. If you are planning to visit Scotland, don't miss the most famous mystery at Loch Ness. The loch, near Inverness, is 37km long and over 200m deep. It is easy to try monster-spotting when travelling along the road which follows one side of the lake. Or you can go in a small submarine and try to find the Loch Ness monster in the depths.

a. ☐

b. ☐

c. ☐

d. ☐

e. ☐

f. ☐

4 *Read the text again and answer the questions.*

a. Where exactly are the Highlands?
b. Why are they called one of Europe's last true wildernesses?
c. What is Scotland famous for?
d. What is Highland Mysteryworld?
e. When was it opened?
f. How much did it cost to build?
g. Where was it built?
h. Who was the Seal Woman?
i. What is Clava Cairns?
j. How long is Loch Ness?
k. Why is it famous?

5 *Look at the pictures on page 37 only. You are presenting a programme on television. Describe the pictures to a friend.*

6 *Read the questions. Then listen and answer them.*

a. Where does Mikis first suggest they go?
b. Where does Karin suggest they go?
c. Why does Mikis say no?
d. Where is the next place Karin suggests they go?
e. How are they going to travel?
f. How long are they going to stay?
g. Why does Karin know about the Highlands?
h. What is Karin going to do now?
i. What is Mikis going to do now?

7 *Write the questions or answers. Then practise the dialogues with a friend.*

A: .... Italy?
B: Maybe. I know they play tennis in France.
A: Well, ...?
B: Yes, they do. Boris Becker is from Germany.

A: Would you like to visit Windsor Castle tomorrow?
B: ....
A: Oh! That's a pity. What about Wednesday?
B: ....
A: Great! Let's meet here at nine o'clock.

A: ....?
B: I can ski very well.
A: ....?
B: Yes, I can. I skate very badly, but I like skating.
A: ....?
B: Tomorrow? I'm afraid I can't, but let's go skating on Friday.

Unit 11a Where was your father born?

1 *Write the names of ten people in your family and your relationship to them.*

▶ *eg* Bill – cousin
Harry – uncle

2 *Write where each person in Exercise 1 was born (you may have to guess). Then add when each person was born. Use these expressions:*

in 1965   about 1965   in the 1960s

3 *Alan's class are preparing family trees. Alan's friend Susan is asking him questions about his relations. Listen and fill in as many first names, places and dates of birth as you can.*

4 *Listen and repeat.*

When was your father born?
He was born in 1950.
She was born about 1945.
Where was he born?
He was born in Calcutta, in India.

5 *Give your friend the names of six of your relations. Then ask and answer.*

▶ *eg* A: Who is Martha?
B: She's my grandmother.
A: When was she born?
B: She was born in the 1930s.
A: Where was she born?
B: I think she was born in Glasgow.

6 *Draw your family tree. Write only your name on the tree. Give it to your friend. Then ask and answer.*

▶ *eg* A: What's your cousin's name?
B: His name's Michael.
A: When and where was he born?
B: I think he was born in Cardiff about 1980.

verb *to be born*: past passive tense p 108   /ɔ:/ **all**

Unit 11b My mother's father's brother!

1 *Look at the photograph.*

How old are the people?
Who is the oldest and who is the youngest?

2 *Susan and Alan are looking at a photograph of some of Alan's relations. Listen, then practise the dialogue.*

3 *Listen and repeat.*

Who is he?
He's my mother's father's brother.

4 *Find out who has got the oldest and youngest relative in your class.*

5 *Look at your friend's family tree. Ask who all the people are.*

► *eg* A: Who's David?
B: He's Peter's cousin.

6 *Fill in the dialogue. Then practise with a friend.*

A: Where ....?
B: I was born in Wales. And you?
A: ....
B: How interesting! And when were you born?
A: ....
B: Really! So was I. I was born in March. When were you born?
A: ....
B: Who is your oldest relative?
A: ....
B: When and where was ...... born?
A: ....
B: Wow! That's very old!
A: ....?
B: My youngest relative is my cousin, Jane. Who is yours?
A: ....

possessive nouns (genitives) p 107 /ð/ mother

Unit 11c A theatrical family

1 *Look at the picture. What is the name of the machine? Work in small groups and ask someone who saw the film to tell you about it.*

2 *Read the text and fill in the missing names and dates in the Barrymore family tree.*

There are many famous kisses in films. One of the kisses that people all over the world remember is in a film made in 1982 when a pretty seven-year-old girl kisses a machine made of plastic and metal. The machine seems to be alive and, of course, the film is *E.T.* – the Extra-Terrestrial.

The little girl was Drew Barrymore who is now a young woman and a very successful actress.

It was no accident that Drew became an actress. She comes from a famous family of actors and actresses. Her great grandfather, Maurice Blythe, was born in India in 1847. In 1872 he started acting in the theatre and used the name Barrymore. All his descendants were born with the surname Blythe but they used the surname Barrymore as their stage name. In 1875 Maurice started acting in the theatre in America. A year later he married Georgiana Emma Drew who was also a theatre actress. Georgiana was born in 1856 and died in 1893. Their son, John Barrymore, was born in 1882 in Philadelphia. Before Maurice died in 1905 he married three times and had several children who became famous actors and actresses in the theatre and then in silent films.

John Barrymore was a very popular actor. His best films were *Dr Jekyll and Mr Hyde* and *Moby Dick*. He married Dolores Costello and, ten years before he died in 1942, their son, John Barrymore Junior, was born.

John Jr started acting in 1950 in the film *The Sundowners*. He made many films but he never became as popular as his father. He married Ildiko Jaid, a Hungarian actress, and in 1975 Drew Barrymore was born.

Drew started acting the year after she was born, when she was only eleven months old, in a television commercial for a dog food. She wanted to be an actress to continue her family tradition. When she was six years old her life changed. She met Steven Spielberg, the famous film director, who chose her for a part in *E.T.* Her performance in the film proved that she was a true Barrymore.

3 *Look at the dates in the family tree and ask and answer with a partner.*

▶ *eg* What happened in 1847?
Maurice Barrymore was born.

4 *Read the text again and write answers to these questions. Compare your answers with a partner.*

▶ *eg* What happened in 1872?
Maurice started acting.

a. What happened in 1875?
b. What happened in 1876?
c. What happened in 1950?
d. What happened in 1976?
e. What happened in 1982?
f. What is Drew's true surname?
g. Why do you think her parents called her Drew?

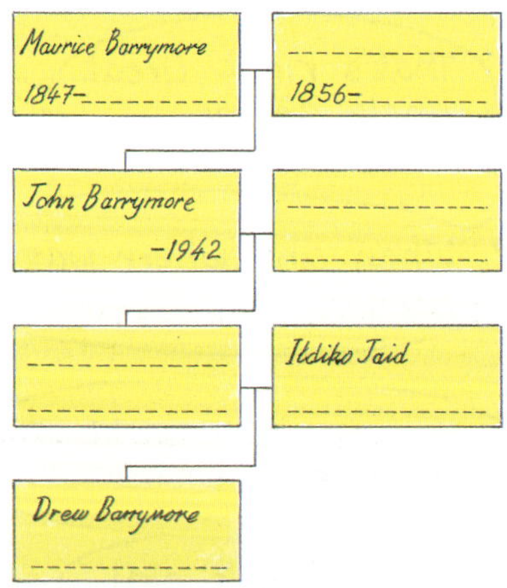

5 *Write about a famous person from your country. Use these ideas:*

date born	parents	brothers/sisters
married	children (names/dates)	date died

verb *to be born*: past passive tense p 108 /dʒ/ George

Unit 11d Who's who?

Unit 11 *Chatterbox A*

Chatterbox B see page *98*.

Susan wrote to Philip, one of Alan's cousins, to ask for some information about his family.

1 *Read Philip's answer and fill in more of the Bailey family tree on page 39.*

Dear Susan,

Thank you for your letter. I think this is the information you want. My name is Philip. I'm 11 years old and I live with my family in Newcastle, in the north of England. I have a brother, William - we call him Bill - and a sister, Mary. We were all born here. My brother and sister are both older than me. My sister was born one year before Bill. My mother was born in London in 1950.

My favourite cousin is Alan. He and his sister were both born in Cardiff and we visit them for our holidays.

My grandparents are very old. Grandfather Donald was born in Manchester in 1901 and he married Grandmother Anne in 1942. She is Irish. She was born in Dublin in 1917.

I have some other cousins. They are called Sally and John. They live in Bristol. Their mother, Aunt Mary, was born in Bristol and their father, my Uncle Freddie, was born in Cardiff in 1944. Aunt Mary died in 1980.

I hope this information helps you.

Best wishes,

Philip

2 *Ask your friend questions and complete the family tree on page 39.*

► *eg* A: What is Alan's sister's name?
B: Her name is Sarah.
A: When was Michael's first son born?
B: He was born in 1978.
A: Where was Michael's wife born?
B: She was born in London.

3 *Answer your friend's questions.*

1 *Read the letter in Chatterbox again. Then write to a pen-friend about your family.*

2 *This is a story about Catherine the Great of Russia's tea-set. Listen to Part One and find the right picture.*

a.

b.

3 *Listen to Part Two. Tick (√) **True** or **False**.*

	True	False
a. Ludmila's father was the director of a museum.	☐	☐
b. Ludmila's father was mayor of Leningrad.	☐	☐
c. Mr Romanov borrowed the tea-set from the museum.	☐	☐
d. It was Mr Sidak's tea-set.	☐	☐
e. Mr Romanov didn't have any glasses for the toast.	☐	☐
f. The first guest threw his teacup on the floor.	☐	☐
g. The other guests threw their teacups on the floor.	☐	☐
h. You can see Catherine's cups, saucers and plates in Leningrad Museum today.	☐	☐

past simple tense p 106, past passive tense *to be born* p 108 /l/ lunch

Unit 12a There's not enough space

1 *Alfonso is talking to Pedro about his bicycle. Listen and tick (√) **True** or **False**. Correct the false statements.*

	True	False
a. Alfonso's got a new bicycle.	☐	☐
b. Pedro doesn't like Alfonso's bike.	☐	☐
c. Alfonso keeps his bike in his garage.	☐	☐
d. Alfonso's father's got a big car.	☐	☐

2 *Listen and repeat.*

There's not enough space.
My dad's car is too big.

3 *Write sentences about the pullover, the T-shirt and the trousers.*

▶ *eg* It's too big.
They're not big enough.

a. .... b. ....
....

4 *James is an artist for Teen Eye. Last week he broke his glasses and then he drew these pictures. Talk to your friend about the pictures. Use these words:*

tall short big small long short fat thin

▶ *eg* A: Look at the boy.
B: Oh, yes. He's too tall.
A: I agree. He's not short enough.

5 *Write a letter to James. Tell him what is wrong with one of the pictures.*

6 *Join these sentences.*

a. The car's not small enough	to drive a car.
b. She's too old	to drink.
c. The coffee's too hot	to go into the garage.
d. He's not old enough	to play with dolls.

7 *Make a list of things you are not old enough or too old to do. Compare your list with a friend.*

too .../not ... enough p 108 /eə/ **chair** /ɪə/ **here**

Unit 12b Each team has got a name

1 *Answer the questions.*

a. Do you play sports at school or with your friends?
b. What sports do you play?
c. Do you usually play sports before or after lunch?
d. Which sports do you play in the winter and which do you play in the summer?
e. Do you have a school sports day? Is this day in the summer or in the winter?

2 *Alfonso wrote Pedro a letter about his school. Read and tick (√)* ***True*** *or* ***False****. Correct the false statements.*

	True	False
a. All the students in Alfonso's class come from Spain.	☐	☐
b. Every girl in his class comes from Spain.	☐	☐
c. All the girls wear badges.	☐	☐
d. On Sports Day all the pupils take part in two sports.	☐	☐
e. Each team does five sports.	☐	☐
f. All the teachers are judges.	☐	☐

I go to a big school in Madrid. Not every pupil in my school comes from Spain. In my class all the boys come from Spain but not all the girls. All the pupils in the school must join one of the sports teams. Each team has got a name. All the boys wear special team ties and every girl wears a special team badge.

Each term there is a Sports Day. There are seven sports to play. Each team must take part in five sports and every pupil must take part in two sports. All the teachers go to the Sports Day but they don't take part in the sports. One teacher from each class is a judge. Last year my team were the school champions.

3 *Listen and repeat.*

Not every pupil comes from Spain.
All the boys wear ties.
Every girl wears a badge.
Each team has got a name.

4 *Ask your friend these questions and write the answers.*

a. How many pupils in your class have got a surname?
All .... a surname.
b. How many blackboards have the classrooms in your school got?
Each .... blackboard.
c. How many pupils in your class are going to do homework tonight?
Every .... tonight!

5 *Ask and answer about Alfonso's letter.*

► *eg* A: How many boys come from Spain?
B: All the boys come from Spain.
A: How often is there a Sports Day?
B: There's a Sports Day each term.

6 *Read Alfonso's letter again, then write about your school and when you play sports.*

Unit 12c Is there much white paper?

1 *Match the food and the containers.*

bar
tin
box
carton
packet
bottle

rice
soup
milk
cooking oil
cereal
chocolate

2 *Look at the pictures in Exercise 1. Ask and answer.*

► *eg* A: How many tins of soup do you have a month?
B: About four a month.
A: How much soup is that?
B: That's two litres.

3 *The Teen Eye team are going to have a meeting this afternoon. Jane and Derek are preparing the room. Listen and tick (√) how much is in the cupboard.*

	a lot of	not much	not many	none
ruled paper				
plain white paper				
blue pens				
black pens				
red pens				

4 *Listen and repeat.*

There's a lot of ruled paper.
Is there much plain white paper?
No, there isn't much.
Are there a lot of pens?
No, there aren't many.
Are there many red pens?
There are a lot of black pens.

5 *Look at the cupboard. Ask and answer.*

Question

Is Are	there	much many a lot of	....	in the cupboard?

Answer

Yes, there	is are	a lot.

No, there	isn't aren't	much. many. a lot.

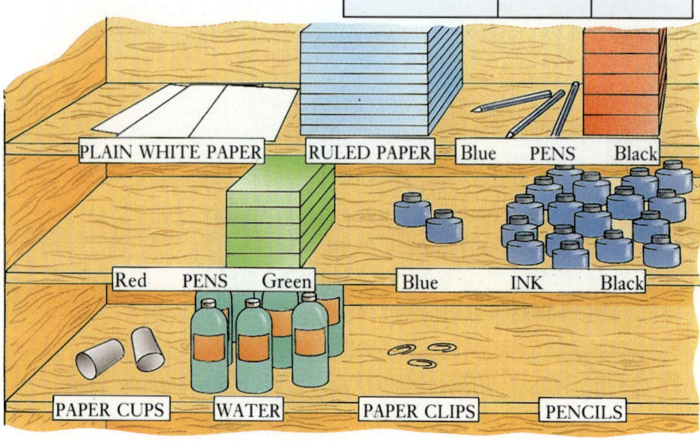

6 *Ask and answer. Use the words in the chart.*

► *eg* A: Do you buy much chocolate?
B: No, I don't buy much but I buy a lot of crisps.
B: Yes, I buy a lot and I buy a lot of crisps too.

Question

Do you	drink buy eat	much many a lot of	tea cups of tea chocolate orange juice sweets etc.	in a	day? week? month? year?

Answer

Yes, No,	I (don't)	drink buy eat	a lot much many	and but I	drink buy eat	a lot of	coffee. cups of coff cola. crisps. packets of cris

7 *Write about your friend.*

► *eg* Peter drinks a lot of cola but he doesn't drink much orange juice. He doesn't eat many bars of chocolate but he eats a lot of sweets.

quantifiers: *much, many, a lot of* p 108 /p/ **p**aper

Unit 12d What are you going as?

There is a fancy dress party for the Teen Eye team tonight.

1 *Answer these questions.*

a. What is a fancy dress party?
b. When did you last go to a fancy dress party?
c. What did you dress up as?
d. What are you going as to your next fancy dress party?
e. Why are you dressing up like that?

2 *Match the names and the costumes.*

1. Zorro
2. Little Red Riding Hood
3. A punk
4. Dracula
5. The Pink Panther
6. Snow White
7. A witch
8. Mickey Mouse

a. ☐

b. ☐

c. ☐

d. ☐

e. ☐

f. ☐

g. ☐

h. ☐

3 *Listen to Alan and Jane and tick (√)* ***True*** *or* ***False****. Correct the false statements.*

	True	False
a. Jane is going to the fancy dress party next Friday.	☐	☐
b. Jane is going as Snow White.	☐	☐
c. Beatrix is dressing up as a cowgirl.	☐	☐
d. Alan is dressing up as a witch.	☐	☐
e. Mikis is going as Dracula.	☐	☐

Unit 12 Chatterbox A

Chatterbox B see page *98*.

1 *Find the secret message! Ask your friend questions and complete the sentences.*

► *eg* A: What do you know about Hollywood?
B: A lot of actors live in Hollywood.

2 *Answer your friend's questions.*

A lot of actors l i ve in Hollywood.
Elephants ___ ___ ___ __ ______ __ ___.
The English don't dr i nk much wine.
Teen Eye __ _ __ _________.
_____ ___' _ ____ _________ __ Finland.
Mosquitoes aren't big en o ugh to break windows.
Pedro __ ___ ______ _ ______ _____
The Portuguese don't smoke much.
There's a lot of milk i n ice-cream.
The Irish _____ _ ___ __ ____.
____ ___ __ the week ____ _ _________ ____.
All children le a rn to speak.
Every country ___ ___ _ _________ ____.
___ Chinese ___ ____.
Amsterdam is i n the Netherlands.
Ice is too c old to eat.
_____ ____' _ ____ ____ __ Italy.

Unit 13a What were you doing?

1 *Number these expressions in the right order of time.*

- ☐ the day before yesterday
- ☐ yesterday evening
- ☐ yesterday morning
- ☐ a fortnight ago
- ☐ a week ago
- ☐ three days ago

2 *Ask a friend where he or she was at the times in Exercise 1.*

▶ *eg* A: Where were you yesterday evening?
B: I was at my friend's house.

3 *Listen to Susan and Alan and answer the questions.*

a. Where was Alan at six o'clock yesterday?
b. What did Susan do at quarter past six yesterday?
c. Why?

At six o'clock I was helping Dan with his homework.

4 *Listen and repeat.*

What were you doing at six o'clock?
I was helping Dan with his homework.
I was doing my homework.

5 *Ask and answer. Use the pictures and the times in the pictures below.*

▶ *eg* A: What was she doing at three o'clock the day before yesterday?
B: She was riding a horse.

6 *Ask and answer about past times.*

▶ *eg* A: What were you doing at six o'clock yesterday evening?
B: I was sleeping.
A: What were you doing at three o'clock last Saturday afternoon?
B: I was visiting my grandmother.

past continuous tense p 109

/ɜː/ bird

Unit 13b Who saw me?

1 *Listen and answer the questions.*

a. Where was Alan at about five o'clock yesterday evening?
b. Who saw him?
c. Was he going home?
d. What was he doing there?
e. Where is Susan's house?

2 *Listen and repeat.*

Who saw me?
Ellen did.
Were you going home?
No, I wasn't.

3 *With a friend write six times on the clocks. Then guess what your friend was doing at these times.*

▶ *eg* A: Were you sleeping at ten o'clock yesterday?
B: No, I wasn't. I was studying at school.

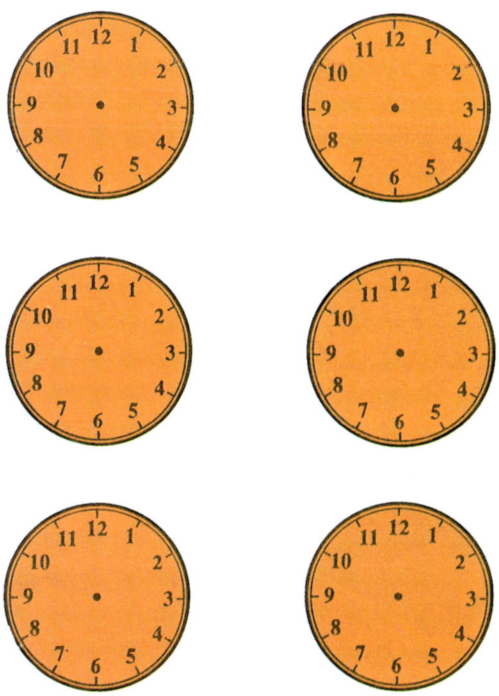

4 *Write sentences.*

▶ *eg* At ten o'clock yesterday my friend Carla wasn't sleeping. She was studying at school.

5 *Read Sarah's secret diary and find the names of all the people. Then ask and answer.*

▶ *eg* A: Who told Sarah there was a basketball match in Dorchester?
B: Peter did.

Peter told me there was a basketball match in Dorchester – our school against Dorchester Secondary School. Mary went with me to see the match. Her father, Donald, drove us there. It was a good match and our team won. My best friend, Caroline, scored 20 points. After the match we had a little party with the other team. Diane, the Dorchester Secondary captain, made cheese sandwiches and Mary opened 30 bottles of Cola. I ate six sandwiches and Mary told me I was getting fat. I must start playing basketball!!

6 *Write the questions and answers.*

Unit 13c What were you doing there?

1 *Answer the questions.*

a. Have you got a library in your school?
b. Where is it?
c. When and why did you last visit it?
d. Have you got a First Aid room in your school?
e. Where is it?
f. When and why did you last visit it?

2 *Read. Then listen and answer.*

Alan goes to school at Cardiff Comprehensive School. It's eleven o'clock in the morning. At ten o'clock this morning there was a big crash. Someone threw a stone at the Headmaster's window. The Headmaster thinks either Alan or his classmate, David, threw the stone. They were not in their classroom at ten o'clock. David and Alan are waiting outside the Headmaster's office.

a. Where was David at ten o'clock this morning?
b. What was he doing?
c. How did he know it was exactly ten o'clock?
d. Where was Alan at ten?
e. What was he doing?
f. How did he know it was exactly ten o'clock?

3 *Listen again and look at the pictures. The Headmaster thinks one of the boys is lying.*

a. Who does he think threw the stone through his window?
b. Why?

4 *Complete the dialogue and practise it with a friend.*

A: What .... last night?
B: I was watching television.
A: Were you watching a cartoon?
B: No, ... I was watching a film and I was eating.
A: What ....?
B: I was eating a pizza and I was drinking.
A: ....?
B: No, I wasn't. I was drinking a cola.
A: .... alone?
B: Yes .... My mother was reading a book.

past continuous tense p 109 /uː/ school /ʊ/ book

Unit 13d A day trip to Newport

1 *Read about Alan's trip to Newport. Where did he have his picnic? Find the right picture.*

Last Thursday Alan and his class went on a day trip to Newport, a town about twenty kilometres from Cardiff. They all met at the school at eight o'clock and waited for the bus. They left Cardiff at 8.30 and arrived in Newport about thirty minutes later.

At Newport they went to a café and had breakfast. Alan had a cup of coffee with milk and a cake. They left the café at 9.45 and went to visit the centre of Newport.

At 10.30 they visited the castle. They stayed there for 45 minutes. Then, at 11.15, they started walking to a special picnic area. It is a special place because there are two rivers there, the Usk and the Severn. The two rivers cross each other. They arrived there at twelve o'clock and they had a picnic lunch on the grass.

At one o'clock they started walking back to the centre of the town. They collected a lot of flowers and leaves to study in class at school in Cardiff.

They arrived in the town at two and went back to the café to have some tea. After tea, at about three o'clock, they got back on the coach and returned to Cardiff. They arrived at half past three.

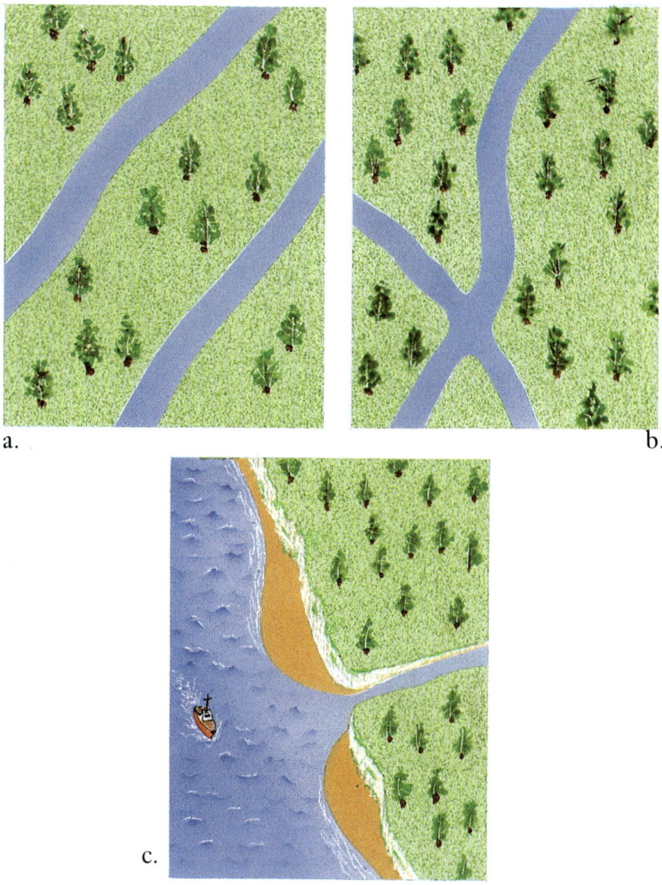

a. b. c.

2 *Read again and answer the questions.*

► *eg* Where was Alan at 8.15 last Thursday? What was he doing?
He was at school. He was waiting for the bus.

1. Where was Alan at 8.45? What was he doing?
2. Where was he at 9.30? What was he doing?
3. Where were they at 10.45? What were they doing?
4. What were they doing at 11.30?
5. Where was Alan at 12.30? What was he doing?
6. What was he doing at 1.30?
7. What was he doing at 2.30?
8. Where were they at 3.15? What were they doing?

3 *Use the information in the answers to Exercise 2 and write the story.*

4 *Read.*

Who went to Newport last week?	Alan's class did.
Who had a cup of coffee?	Alan did.

5 *Ask your partners questions and find out who did these things.*

	name
a. saw you first this morning	......
b. watched TV last night	......
c. walked to school this morning	......
d. had tea for breakfast today	......

Unit 13 *Chatterbox A*

Chatterbox B see page *99*.

1 *Read the story and ask your friend for the missing names.*

► *eg* A: Who went to the cinema with Beatrix and Karin?
B: Mikis did.

2 *Answer your friend's questions.*

Last Friday afternoon Mikis, Beatrix and Karin went to the cinema. .... and Beatrix met at the Teen Eye offices and Karin waited at the cinema.
.... and .... liked the film very much. After the film they all went to Hamburger Heaven. Mikis had a hamburger. .... had a cheeseburger and Beatrix had a fishburger. Beatrix and Karin drank water and Mikis had a cola.
In the evening they went to Jane's house and .... and .... played cards. Beatrix watched television and .... wrote a letter to her mother.
At about eight o'clock .... took Beatrix home in her car and Mikis went home by bus. .... telephoned for a taxi.

Unit 14a What did you have to study?

1 *Have you got any problems at school? Add two subjects. Then number them using the key.*

☐ Maths ☐ History ☐ English

☐ Geography ☐ Art ☐ Your mother-tongue

☐ .... ☐ ....

Key: [0] No problems [1] A few problems

[2] A lot of problems [3] One big problem

2 *Ask a friend.*

a. Did you have to do extra study last year?
b. What did you have to study?
c. How many extra hours did you have to do?
d. Do you have to do extra study this year?
e. What do you have to study?
f. How many extra hours do you have to study?

3 *Listen to Alan and his friend, Jerry. Then answer these questions.*

a. Did Jerry play handball last Thursday?
b. Why not?
c. Is Jerry going to play handball this afternoon?
d. Why not?

4 *Listen and repeat.*

Did you have to do extra homework?
Yes, I did. I had to do twenty extra exercises.
I didn't have to do extra history.

5 *Ask and answer. Use the subjects in Exercise 1.*

▶ *eg* A: Did you have to do extra maths?
B: Yes, I did.
A: When did you have to do it?
B: On Wednesday.

6 *What did you have to do and not have to do each day last week? Write your answers.*

▶ *eg* On Sunday I had to visit my aunt but I didn't have to go to school.

7 *Ask and answer about last week. Use your answers to Exercise 6.*

▶ *eg* A: What did you have to do last Sunday?
B: I had to visit my aunt.
A: What didn't you have to do?
B: I didn't have to go to school.

8 *Tell another friend about your friend.*

▶ *eg* Carla had to write invitations to her party but she didn't have to buy stamps.

9 *Divide into small groups and discuss.*

What was the last sport you played?
What did you and your friends have to do before you started the game/match?

▶ *eg* I had to buy special shoes.

past obligation: *had to* p 109

/h/ **h**omework

Unit 14b What did you have to do?

1 *Read these instructions from an examination paper. Answer the questions.*

a. Do you think it's from a geography, maths, language or history exam? Why?
b. How long is the exam altogether?
c. How many words do you have to write in the Composition part?

GRAMMAR Questions 1–8
Maximum time: 1 hour
There are eight questions.
You **MUST** answer questions 1 and 3.
You must answer three other questions.

COMPOSITION Questions 9–10
Maximum time: half an hour
Minimum number of words: 100
You must either write a letter (Q.9) or a story (Q.10).

2 *Write the rules for an English test you took recently. Include instructions about these points.*

a. Did Mikis have to write a story?
b. How many grammar questions did he have to answer?

3 *Ask and answer about the rules of the test.*

How many questions did you have to answer?
I had to answer six.

4 *Ask and answer about the things Mikis had to do during the examination. Ask about:*

grammar questions   composition   number of words
letter or story

▶ *eg* A: Which grammar questions did he have to answer?
B: He had to answer questions 1 and 3.

5 *Write the words in the correct order. Then practise the dialogue.*

Bill: Why didn't you come to the party last Friday?
(you to party didn't the last why come Friday)
John: ....
(to had 8 o'clock I go bed at to)
Bill: ....?
(did why early to so bed you go)
John: I ....
because ....
(early to to had I bed go because examination on had morning I an Saturday)
Bill: ....?
(the difficult was examination?)
John: ....
(it yes was)
Bill: ....?
(you pass did it?)
John: ....
(wasn't I passed because it tired yes I)

6 *Write the rules for an English test you took recently. Include instructions about these points.*

number of questions to answer   using dictionaries   silence
leaving the room   maximum time

7 *Ask and answer about the rules of the test.*

▶ *eg* A: Did you have to write on only one side of the paper?
B: Yes, I did./No, I didn't.
A: How many questions did you have to answer?
B: I had to answer six questions.

Unit 14c Which sport?

Fatma is in Greece. She is preparing a programme about the history of the Olympic Games.

1 *Match the words and the pictures.*

Throwing:

1. javelin
2. hammer
3. discus

Jumping:

4. pole vault
5. long jump
6. high jump
7. hurdles

2 *Answer these questions.*

a. Which of the sports in Exercise 1 do you do?
b. Which is your favourite?
c. There are six field events and one track event in the pictures. Which one is the track event?

3 *Listen to Fatma talking to Mikis about the athletics camp. Number the pictures in the right order.*

4 *Listen again and answer the questions.*

a. What events does Mikis like?
   Field: ....
   Track: ....

b. What did he have to do at the athletics camp?
   .... (get up)
   .... (stand)

c. What did the two groups have to do before breakfast?
   Field group: ....
   Track group: ....

d. When they returned to the camp, what did they have to do before breakfast?
   ....

e. What did they do during the day?
   ....

f. What was Mikis's favourite time of the day?
   ....

g. What did he do at this time?
   ....

5 *Mikis wrote a postcard to Derek from the athletics camp. You are Mikis. Write the postcard.*

past obligation: *had to* p 109, past simple tense p 106   /m/ ha**mm**er

Unit 14d Disaster in Sorrento

1 *What do you know about Italy? Answer these questions.*

a. Sorrento is a small town in Italy. Is it in the north or the south?
b. What is Pompeii?
c. What is Mount Vesuvius?

2 *Read and answer these questions.*

a. How many disasters were there?
b. What did Fatma have to do? Why?

Every year the International Satellite Association has a conference for its members. The conference in 1989 in Sorrento, Italy, was terrible. There were a lot of disasters.

The members from England all travelled on a special train from London to Gatwick airport, but they had to wait a long time at a station between London and Gatwick because there was an accident. There was a lot of fog and the plane took off and arrived at Naples airport, near Sorrento, nearly eight hours late.

A lot of the people had food poisoning and went to bed for the conference. Two members broke their legs. A snake bit Fatma and she had to go to hospital.

There is always a golf competition during the conference, but there was no golf course in Sorrento and the competition had to be cancelled.

The climax of all the disasters was during the final ceremony. An Italian member decided to fly over all the members and drop 3,500 roses on them. He flew over them five times but not one rose landed in Sorrento. Residents living near Mount Vesuvius were very surprised to see thousands of roses all over the volcano!

3 *Look at the pictures and number them in the right order.*

a. ☐ Where? Why?

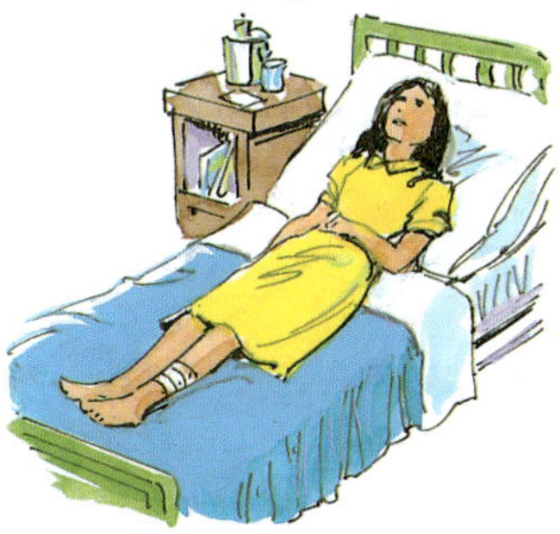

b. ☐ Where? Why?

c. ☐ Who? Where?

d. ☐ What?

e. ☐ What?

f. ☐ What?

4 *Ask your friend questions about the pictures. Use the words under the pictures.*

5 *Make a list of all the things that went wrong.*

Unit 14 Chatterbox A

Chatterbox B see page 99.

1 *Look at the note from Alan's mum about cleaning his untidy room. Ask your friend questions and fill in the note.*

► *eg* A: What did he have to put on the bedside table?
B: He had to put the clock there.
A: Where did he have to put the clock?
B: He had to put it on the bedside table.

Alan

Before you go out you

MUST

put the

clock	–	bedside table
records	–	shelf
....	–	bookcase
shirts	–	drawer
....	–	wardrobe
shoes	–	....
school bag	–	chair
pen / pencils	–	....
posters	–	wall
....	–	school bag
ties	–	wardrobe
socks	–	drawer

Mum

2 Answer your friend's questions.

Unit 15 Language check

Teen Eye on the Symbol of Portugal

1 *Look at the picture and answer these questions.*

a. What kind of bird is it?
b. What sound does it make?
c. When does it make the sound?

2 *Look at the pictures below. Describe one of the pictures. Your friend must guess which one.*

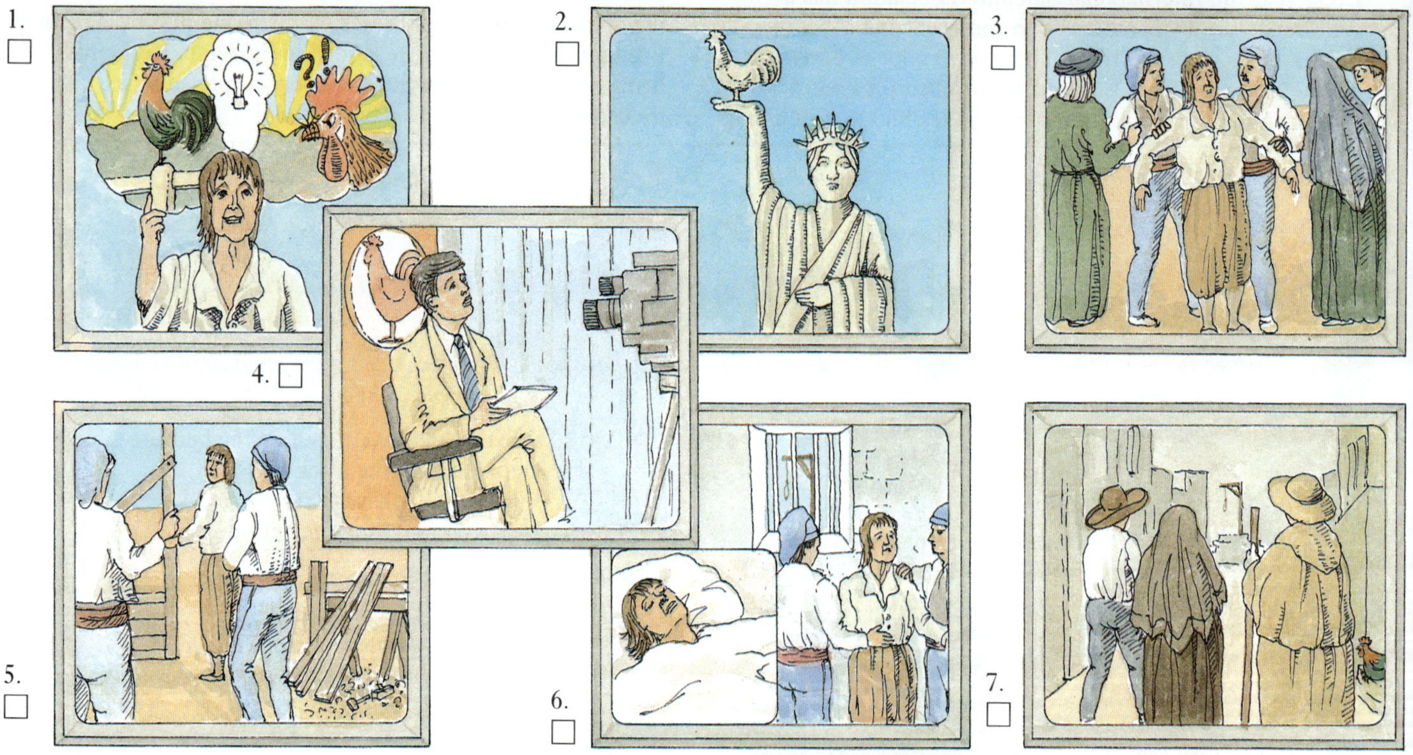

3 *Read the paragraphs and match them with the pictures. Then put the paragraphs in order.*

A All the people in the village laughed. They didn't believe him. 'A cock crows every morning and it's going to crow tomorrow morning,' they said.

B Good afternoon, everybody. This is Martin Hall, your host for today's Teen Eye programme. Today we're in Lisbon, the capital of Portugal. Derek Farley visited the city and discovered a fascinating story about the cock – the animal you can see all over Portugal in toy and tourist shops. The cock is the symbol of Portugal. Derek discovered why.

C The next morning all the villagers got up before dawn to listen to the cock and to see Antonio executed.

D 'When the shopkeeper was killed I was sleeping at home,' said Antonio. The police didn't believe him and they decided to execute him the next morning. Antonio was very worried and afraid.

E Then Antonio had an idea. There was a cock in the village and every morning it crowed at dawn. 'I am innocent!' he shouted. 'To prove it, the cock isn't going to crow tomorrow morning!'

F But the cock didn't crow, and the police and the villagers believed Antonio. The cock became the symbol of justice because it helped to show that Antonio was innocent and it is now the symbol of Portugal.

G One day many years ago Antonio, a carpenter, had to go to Barcelos, a small Portuguese town. While he was working in Barcelos, the police arrested him for killing a shopkeeper.

4 *Cover the story on page 55 and look at the pictures. Tell the story to your friend.*

5 *What is the symbol of your town or country and why? Talk about it with your teacher and friends and write a paragraph about it.*

6 *Fatma is talking to Bill, the doorman at the Teen Eye offices. Listen and answer the questions.*

a. Where was Bill at eleven o'clock last Friday?
b. What was he doing?
c. Where was Fatma at eleven o'clock last Friday?
d. What did she have to do?
e. Why?
f. How many injections did she have?
g. Where did she have them?

7 *Write the story. Use your answers to Exercise 6.*

8 *Write the questions or answers. Then practise the dialogues with a friend.*

a. A: ....?
B: I was born in Florence.
A: ....?
B: Yes, that's right. It's in Italy.

b. A: Why aren't you drinking your coffee?
B: ....
A: Why don't you put some more milk in it?
B: ....

c. A: Somebody told me it's your birthday tomorrow.
B: ....?
A: Pamela did.

d. A: ....?
B: No, there isn't much sugar. I must buy some more.
A: ....?
B: Yes, there are a lot of biscuits.
A: ....?
B: No, not many people. Just some friends from school.

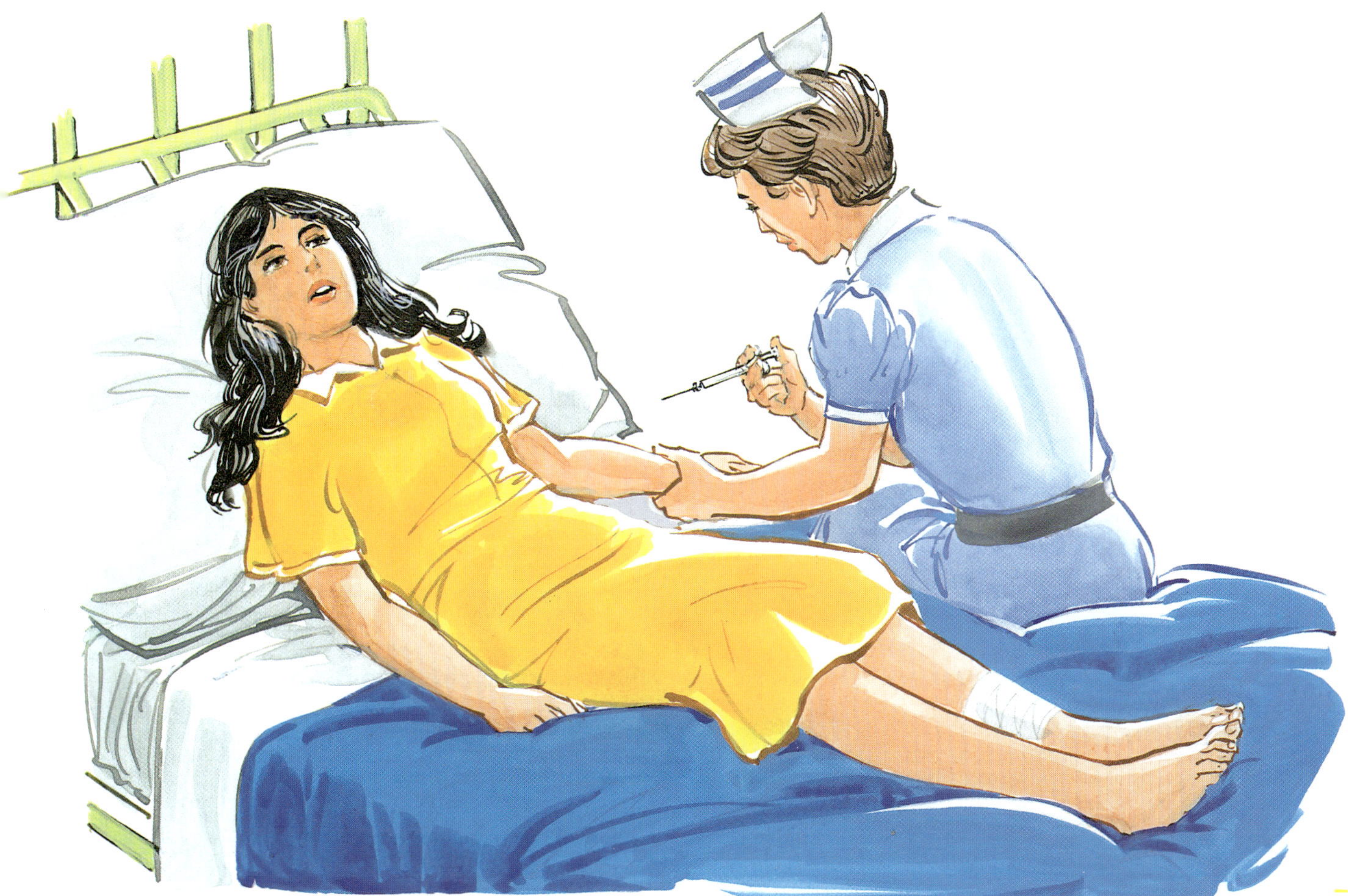

Unit 16a I can't see anything!

1 *Answer these questions.*

a. What is fog?
b. Do you have fog in your country?
c. If yes, which areas have a lot of fog?
d. Which months of the year are foggy?

2 *Derek and Fatma are driving home in a very thick fog. Listen and tick (√) **True** or **False**. Correct the false statements.*

	True	False
a. Fatma is driving.	☐	☐
b. The car hits a man on a bicycle.	☐	☐
c. The dustbin is in the middle of the road.	☐	☐
d. The car hits a dustbin.	☐	☐

3 *Listen and repeat.*

I can't see anything.
There's something on the left.
There's nothing there.
I can't see anybody.

4 *Look at the picture. Ask and answer.*

► *eg* A: Can you see anything behind that tree?
B: I can see something but I don't know what it is.
A: Can you see anybody near that tree?
B: I can see somebody but I don't know who it is.

5 *Look at the pictures. Then read the sentences and fill in the missing words.*

Paul: There's (a.) .... over there!
Alan: Yes, I can see (b.) .... but I don't know what it is.

Sally: Is there (c.) .... on television tonight?
Sue: No, there's (d.) .... good on.

Mark: Look, there's (e.) .... by the front door. It's a man.
David: I can't see (f.) ....
Mark: Yes, there he is. Look again.
David: There's (g.) .... there. It's the shadow of a tree.

indefinite pronouns p 109 /ɒ/ lost

Unit 16b It isn't as big as yours!

1 *Françoise is visiting Beatrix in Amsterdam for the first time. She is in Beatrix's house. Listen and tick (√)* ***True*** *or* ***False****. Correct the false statements.*

	True	False
a. Françoise doesn't like Beatrix's bedroom.	☐	☐
b. Beatrix's bedroom is comfortable.	☐	☐
c. Beatrix likes riding horses.	☐	☐
d. Françoise doesn't like Michael Jackson.	☐	☐

2 *Listen and repeat.*

It isn't as big as your bedroom.
My records aren't as new as yours.

3 *Look at the picture. Then read the sentences and fill in the missing names.*

a. Jane is as tall as ....
b. Beatrix isn't as tall as Françoise but she isn't as short as ....
c. Karin isn't as thin as Françoise but she isn't as fat as ....
d. .... hair isn't as short as Françoise's but it isn't as long as Beatrix's.

4 *Write sentences about the boys like the ones in Exercise 3.*

5 *Read the sentences then match the prices and the fruit.*

The pears aren't as cheap as the bananas and the oranges aren't as expensive as the apples. The bananas are as expensive as the apples.

Fruit

Price tag

Unit 16c It's as good as this one

1 *In pairs join these adjectives to the subjects they can describe. Some adjectives can describe different subjects. Change pairs and compare.*

good	animals
tasty	sports
exciting	clothes
elegant	films
talented	food
smart	books
affectionate	singers
big	hobbies
aggressive	school subjects
long	drinks

2 *Listen to Derek and Jane. Write who the presents are for.*

who for	presents	adjectives
....	bag	good
....	dictionary	exciting
....	book	warm
....	scarf	expensive
		big
		long
		heavy

3 *Listen again and link the adjectives to the presents they describe.*

4 *Complete the table with things you like a little and things you like a lot.*

	like a little	like a lot
sports		
animals		
clothes		
films		
books		
school subjects		
singers		
hobbies		
....		
....		
....		

5 *In pairs ask and answer. Include some of the adjectives from Exercise 1.*

▶ *eg* What sports do you like?
I like football but it isn't as interesting as athletics.
What food do you like?
I like English cheese but it isn't as tasty as French cheese.

6 *Compare the beds. Use these words:*

high	low	expensive	cheap	wide	narrow
long	short	big	small	light	heavy

▶ *eg* The Dream bed isn't as wide as the Royal bed.

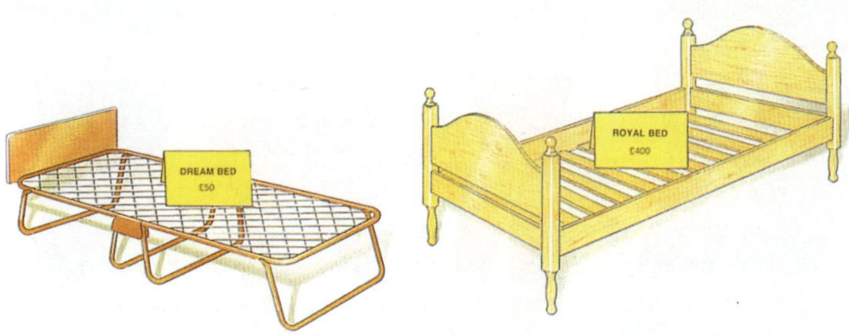

comparatives: *as* ... *as* p 109 /uː/ blue

Unit 16d Martial arts

1 *Look at the pictures. Four of the sports are martial art sports. Match the names of the sports and the pictures.*

1. Kendo
2. Judo
3. Karate
4. Wrestling
5. Fencing
6. Sumo

a. ☐

b. ☐

c. ☐

d. ☐

e. ☐

f. ☐

2 *Read the story about martial arts. Then make notes about what happened at the times in the chart.*

Dates	Notes
Seventeenth century	
Eighteenth century	
Nineteenth century	
1882	
1920s	

Japanese martial arts are methods of self-defence and fighting. They began in Japan and became sports at the end of the nineteenth century. Martial arts come from very old techniques of fighting. One of these techniques is jiu-jitsu. Jiu-jitsu is a method of fighting hand to hand, using as few weapons as possible. The fighting people, or samurai, developed it in Japan during the seventeenth century. Jiu-jitsu includes methods of hitting, kicking, throwing, choking and holding the person you are fighting with.

Typical martial arts are judo, karate, aikido, sumo and kendo. Judo is a type of wrestling based on jiu-jitsu methods of not using weapons. Judo wrestlers wear special white jackets. In 1882 a man called Jigoro Kano opened the first school of judo and started it as a sport. Sumo, or belt wrestling, also began with the samurai.

Karate is another method of fighting without weapons. It became a sport in the 1920s. Karate is as difficult as judo. Feet and hands are very important. The basic difference between karate and judo is that in karate you do not try to throw the other person. Aikido is a method of self-defence similar to judo.

Kendo is a kind of fencing. It began in the eighteenth century as sword fighting practice. The samurai used light bamboo swords because they didn't want to kill each other when they practised! Practising sword fighting became very popular and the sport was born.

3 *Use your notes and write the story of the development of Japanese martial arts.*

Unit 16 Chatterbox A

Chatterbox B see page *100*.

1 *Look at the picture of the Suny television and fill in the chart. Then answer your friend's questions.*

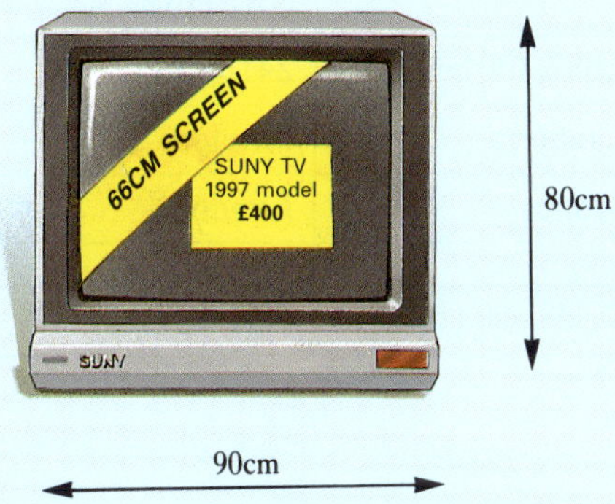

2 *Ask your friend questions about the Ati television and fill in the chart.*

► *eg* A: How wide is the Ati TV?
B: It's eighty centimetres wide.

Television	wide	high	cost	year model	screen size
Suny					
Ati					

3 *Complete these sentences using* ***is*** *or* ***isn't****.*

a. The Suny television .... as new as the Ati.
b. The Ati television .... as high as the Suny.
c. The Suny television .... as cheap as the Ati.
d. The Ati television .... as wide as the Suny.
e. The Suny screen .... as big as the Ati.

4 *Read your sentences to your friend. Are your sentences the same?*

Unit 17a Bigger and better

1 *Answer these questions about your country.*

a. How big is it? ....
b. How many people are there? ....
c. How long do men/women live for? ....
d. How much do these things cost?
   a cup of coffee ....   a record ....
   a sandwich ....   a cinema ticket ....
   a soft drink ....   a bicycle ....
e. What is your country famous for? ....

2 *Look at these tables. Read about Australia and Britain then put these headings beside the right table.*

Population   **Cost of living**   **Land**   **Health**

a. ....

	Australia	**United Kingdom (Britain)**
Area	7,682,300 km^2	241,000 km^2
Capital	Canberra	London
Largest city	Sydney	London

b. ....

	17,938,500 (1994)	58,395,000 (1994)

c. ....
Life expectancy

Men	73.2 (1994)	73 (1994)
Women	80.0 (1994)	78 (1994)

d. ....

soft drinks	$1.00	45p
cup of coffee	$1.30	£1.00
record	$18.00	£8.24
sandwich	$1.65	£1.30
touring bicycle	$220	£375
cinema ticket	$11.00	£5.00

Currency: Aus $1 = 100 cents = UK 50p
UK £1 = Aus $2

3 *Listen. Number the topics in the order you hear them.*

☐ land size   ☐ cost of living   ☐ health
☐ population   ☐ weather

4 *Listen and repeat.*

Britain is smaller than Australia.
Britain has a bigger population than Australia.
Do people live longer in Britain than in Australia?
The weather is better in Australia.
Coffee is cheaper but a record is more expensive.

5 *Ask and answer. Use the information in Exercise 2.*

▶ *eg* A: Is Britain smaller than Australia?
B: Yes, it is.
A: Do women in Britain live longer than women in Australia?
B: No, they don't.

6 *Read. Then write the number of syllables in each word.*

small   has got 1 syllable
hap'py   has got 2 syllables
ex'pen'sive   has got 3 syllables

a. ☐ long   e. ☐ beautiful   h. ☐ light
b. ☐ fat   f. ☐ heavy   i. ☐ cheap
c. ☐ tall   g. ☐ difficult   j. ☐ friendly
d. ☐ popular

7 *Read. Then fill in the gaps.*

1 or 2 syllables → adjective + **er** + **than**
▶ *eg* smaller than
3 or more syllables → **more** + adjective + **than**
▶ *eg* more expensive than

a. Buy the blue one. It's .cheaper.. (cheap)
b. I want the pink flowers. They're .... than the yellow ones. (beautiful)
c. Let's go to the Star Disco. It's .... than Gringo's. (popular)
d. She's a good basketball player because she's .... than the others. (tall)
e. I like Robert. He's .... than the others. (friendly)
f. I don't like that book. It's .... than the first one. (difficult)

8 *Write about your country. Compare it to Australia.*

comparative adjectives: –*er* + *than*, *more* ... *than* p 109   /ə/ bigger

Unit 17b The wallaby is smaller

1 *Which is the kangaroo and which is the wallaby?*

a. ....

Height	....
Weight	....
Colour	....
Tail	....
Country	....

Height	....
Weight	....
Colour	....
Tail	....
Country	....

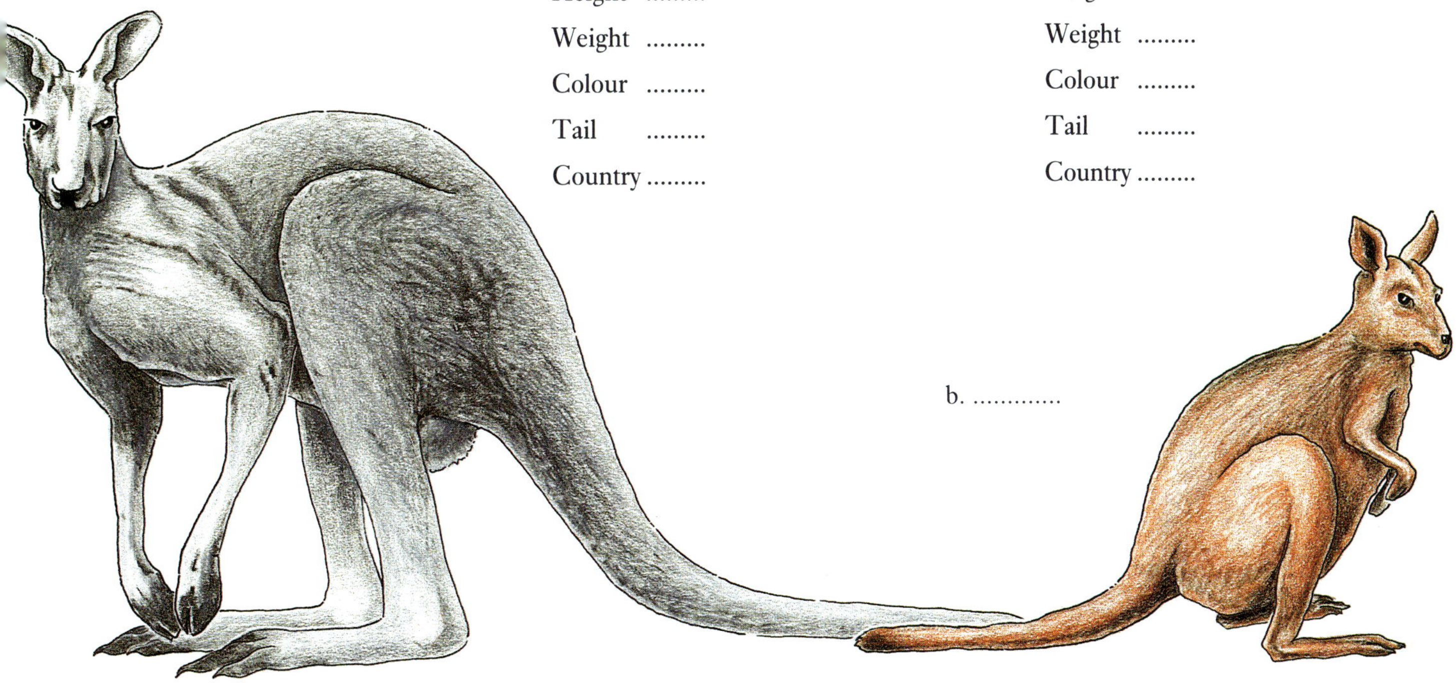

b. ....

2 *Read. Then fill in the charts in Exercise 1.*

The kangaroo and the wallaby

The kangaroo and the wallaby look alike. They are from the same family. The kangaroo is more well-known because it is the national symbol of Australia. The kangaroo is about 1.8 metres tall and weighs about 45 kilos. The wallaby is smaller. It is about 1 metre tall and weighs about 23 kilos. Kangaroos are usually red or grey. Wallabies are grey or brown. The kangaroo has a tail which is about 1.2 metres long. The wallaby's tail is shorter. It is about 75 cm long. The wallaby and the kangaroo can run very fast. They can both run about 50 kilometres per hour. Wallabies are friendlier than kangaroos and are very popular in zoos and parks.

3 *Read again, then answer these questions.*

a. Which animal is larger?
b. Which animal has a longer tail?
c. Which animal is more popular?
d. Which animal is smaller?
e. Which animal is heavier?

4 *Find the opposite adjective. Then write the comparative forms for each adjective.*

► *eg* fat – thin fatter thinner
friendly – unfriendly more friendly more unfriendly

		comparatives
fat	small	....
cheap	good	....
stupid	thin	....
beautiful	unfriendly	....
hot	ugly	....
large	expensive	....
bad	short	....
friendly	light	....
long	clever	....
big	difficult	....
heavy	small	....
easy	cold	....

Unit 17c Which do you prefer?

1 *Match the dialogue and the picture.*

1. A: Do you prefer jogging or swimming?
   B: Well, I prefer jogging because it's easier.
   A: Not me. I like swimming better.
   B: Why?
   A: Because it's more enjoyable.

2. A: Which kind of fruit do you prefer? Apples or oranges?
   B: I prefer apples because they are easier to eat.
   A: And you?
   B: I like oranges better because they are sweeter.

3. A: Which game do you prefer? Cards or chess?
   B: I like chess better because it's more interesting.
   A: I don't. I like playing cards better.
   B: Why?
   A: Because the games are shorter!

a. ☐

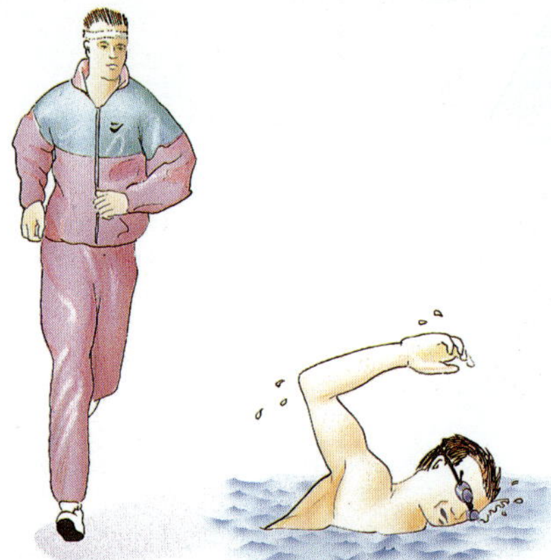

b. ☐

c. ☐

2 *Listen and repeat.*

Do you prefer swimming or jogging?
I prefer jogging because it's easier.
I like swimming better.
Which kind of fruit do you prefer?

3 *Practise the dialogues in Exercise 1. Then make these changes and practise the new dialogues.*

Dialogue 1: jogging/swimming → playing tennis/playing volleyball
Dialogue 2: apples/oranges → bananas/pears
Dialogue 3: cards/chess → bingo/Monopoly

4 *Find the pairs. Then tick (✓) your preference in each pair and write the reason for your preference.*

Some useful comparatives
shorter stronger sweeter easier fresher hotter longer colder
more exciting enjoyable interesting natural refreshing

....	☐	coffee	summer	☐	....
....	☐	tennis	juice	☐	....
sweeter	☑	cola	tea	☐	....
....	☐	cheese sandwich	golf	☐	....
....	☐	geography	westerns	☐	....
....	☐	horror films	snow	☐	....
....	☐	autumn	jam sandwich	☐	....
....	☐	sun	history	☐	....

5 *Practise this dialogue for each pair in Exercise 4.*

A: Which do you prefer? Cola or juice?
B: I prefer cola.
A: Why?
B: Because it's sweeter.

6 *Write five sentences about your friend. Say why your friend prefers something.*

► *eg* She prefers cola to juice because it's sweeter.

present simple tense p 105 /ɔɪ/ boy

Unit 17d Taronga Zoo

1 *Look at the pictures in Exercise 2. Describe one of them. Your friend must guess which one.*

2 *Linda Rose is at Taronga Zoo in Sydney, Australia. Listen and write the names of these animals under the correct pictures.*

emu wombat kookaburra duck-billed platypus

a. Name ....
Length ....
Bill ....
Colour ....
Lifestyle ....

b. Name ....
Height ....
Weight ....
Speed ....
Lifestyle ....

c. Name ....
Length ....
Weight ....
Bill ....
Feet ....

d. Name ....
Length ....
Weight ....
Lifestyle ....

3 *Listen again and fill in the information about the animals.*

4 *Tick (√) the sentences **True** or **False**. Correct the false statements.*

	True	False
a. The Taronga Zoo only takes injured animals.	☐	☐
b. Many animals in Taronga Zoo were born there.	☐	☐
c. The kookaburra lives in the water.	☐	☐
d. Kookaburras live in families.	☐	☐
e. The emu is smaller than the kookaburra.	☐	☐
f. The emu runs faster than the kangaroo.	☐	☐
g. The duck-billed platypus lives in trees.	☐	☐
h. The wombat has a long tail.	☐	☐

5 *Listen and repeat.*

The emu is about 1.5 metres tall.
The duck-billed platypus is about 61 centimetres long.
The wombat weighs up to 27 kilos.

6 *Ask and answer about the animals in Exercise 2.*

► *eg* A: How long is a kookaburra?
B: It's 47 centimetres long.
A: How tall is an emu?
B: It's about 1.5 metres tall.

7 *Ask and answer about your height and weight. Then find the average age, height and weight in your class.*

Unit 17 Chatterbox A

Chatterbox B see page *100*.

1 *Ask your friend questions about the Asian elephant. Fill in the chart.*
How tall/How heavy/How wide/What colour

2 *Answer your friend's questions about the African elephant.*

3 *Prepare and give a one-minute talk about the difference between an African and an Asian elephant.*

African elephant

Height: 3.5 metres
Weight: 5,440–6,350 kg
Colour: dark grey – some have pink on their ears
Ears: 1.2 metres wide
Origin: the grasslands of Africa

Asian elephant

Height: ....
Weight: ....
Colour: ....
....
....
Origin: ....
....
....

Unit 18a Which is the richest country?

1 *Complete the chart.*

Adjective	Comparative	Superlative	A
big	bigger	biggest	√
	smaller		
		richest	
high			
long			
poor			
	taller		
short			

2 *Listen to Pedro and Jane. In column A, tick (√) the superlative adjectives you hear.*

3 *Listen and repeat.*

Which is the richest country in the world?
The richest country in the world is Bermuda.

4 *Ask a friend questions and fill in the chart. Choose your answers from the list. The answers are at the end of Unit 18c.*

► *eg* Which is the richest country in the world?
What is the name of the highest mountain in the world?
Where do the tallest people in the world live?

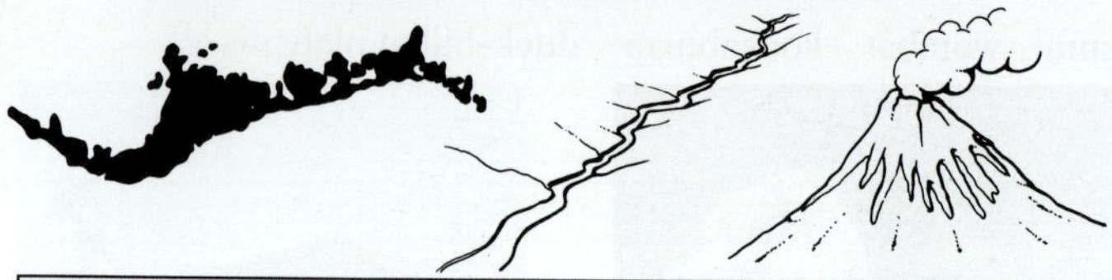

Which country?	What's the name?	Where do they live?
richest Bermuda	highest mountain	tallest
smallest	highest volcano	shortest
biggest	longest river	
poorest	shortest river	

Answers	
Bermuda	Chad
Rwanda and Burundi	The Nile
Mount Everest	The D River in America
The Vatican	Russia
Cerro Aconcagua in Argentina	Zaire

5 *Look at the pictures of the Teen Eye team on page 58. Ask and answer to find the tallest, shortest, fattest and thinnest, and the ones with the longest and shortest hair.*

► *eg* A: Who is the tallest boy?
B: Mikis is.

6 *In groups find out the biggest and smallest in your country and the tallest and shortest in your school or families.*

► *eg* A: Which is the biggest city in the Netherlands?
B: The biggest city in the Netherlands is Amsterdam.
A: Who is the shortest teacher in the school?
B: The science teacher is the shortest teacher in the school.

Country	**School/family**
city	teacher
forest	student
natural park	father
building	mother
university	brother
river	sister

regular superlative adjectives p 109 /tʃ/ rich

Unit 18b Peter drinks the least

1 *Read the text and fill in the names in the chart.*

Alan drinks more milk than Peter each week and Susan drinks the most. Alan drinks less milk than Susan and Peter drinks the least. Susan eats fewer potatoes than Peter and Alan eats the fewest. Peter is better at geography than Alan and Susan is the best. Peter is worse at geography than Susan but Alan is the worst.

Name	Milk	Potatoes	Geography
....	1 litre	3 kilos	7/10
....	2 litres	1 kilo	4/10
....	3 litres	2 kilos	9/10

2 *Read again. Then find and write the comparative and superlative adjectives.*

Comparative	Superlative
more	most
....	....
....	....
....	....
....	....

3 *Draw a chart like the one in Exercise 1. Choose a drink, a countable food and a school subject. Write in your name and the names of two friends. Ask questions and fill in the chart.*

► *eg* How much .... do you drink each week?
How many .... do you eat each week?
What is your .... mark?

4 *Write sentences about you and your friends. Use the text in Exercise 1 as a model.*

5 *Look at the pictures of Tom and Harry. Write the missing words.*

	Tom	Harry
jacket	longer	shorter
buttons	....	more
pockets	....	....
mouth	larger	....
hair	less	....
nose	....	smaller
feet	....	....
trousers	....	....
eyes	....	....

6 *Write sentences about Tom and Harry.*

► *eg* Tom's jacket is longer than Harry's.
Harry's jacket has got more buttons than Tom's.

7 *Look at the pictures again and ask your friend questions.*

► *eg* A: Who's got the longest jacket?
B: Tom has.
A: Who's got the most buttons?
B: Harry has.

Unit 18c Gatwick Airport

1 *Answer these questions.*

a. What is the name of the nearest airport to your city?
b. How old is it?
c. What happens at an airport?

2 *Listen to part of a radio programme about Gatwick Airport, in the south of England. Number the adjectives in the order you hear them.*

☐ fewest
☐ biggest
☐ most
☐ tallest
☐ most popular
☐ most frequent
☐ more dangerous
☐ less

3 *Listen again and answer.*

a. Is Gatwick the biggest airport in the world?
b. Who ask the fewest questions?
c. What are the most popular questions?
d. Why is Gatwick a dangerous airport?
e. How long does it take fire engines to get to any part of the airport?

4 *Use the information in Exercises 2 and 3 and write a paragraph about Gatwick Airport.*

Answers to Unit 18a, Exercise 4.

Which is the	biggest smallest richest poorest	country in the world?	Russia The Vatican Bermuda Chad
Where do the	tallest shortest	people in the world live?	Rwanda and Burundi Zaire
What is the name of the	highest mountain highest volcano longest river shortest river	in the world?	Mount Everest Cerro Aconcagua The Nile The D River

regular and irregular superlative adjectives p 109 /əʊ/ most

Unit 18d It's the highest mountain

1 *Read about three islands in the Mediterranean. Then make a chart comparing the three islands.*

Cyprus has a population of about 702,000 people. The island covers an area of 9,267 square kilometres and is 75 kilometres wide and 330 kilometres long. It rains about 39 centimetres each year and the average temperature is 24.8°C. The highest mountain is Mount Olympus. It is 1,953 metres high.

Sardinia is an island in the Mediterranean sea near Italy. It has an area of 24,092 square kilometres. The highest mountain is Mount Gennargentu which is 1,834 metres high. The island is about 265 kilometres long and 145 kilometres wide and has a population of about one and a half million. The average temperature is about 17 °C and it rains 47.9 centimetres every year.

Mount Cinto is in the north of Corsica. It is 2,710 metres high. Corsica covers 8,720 square kilometres and is about 184 kilometres long and 55 kilometres wide. About 275,000 people live on the island. The average temperature is about 16 °C and it rains 51 centimetres every year.

2 *Write a paragraph comparing the islands. Use comparative and superlative adjectives.*

Unit 18 Chatterbox A

Chatterbox B see page *101*.

1 *Ask your friend questions and fill in the chart.*

► *eg* A: How many eggs does the average Briton eat each year?
B: The average Briton eats 236 eggs each year.

2 *Answer your friend's questions.*

Nationalities			
		Singular	*Plural*
Britain	=	Briton	the British
France	=	Frenchman/woman	the French
Italy	=	Italian	the Italians
Russia	=	Russian	the Russians
Australia	=	Australian	the Australians
Japan	=	Japanese	the Japanese
Ireland	=	Irishman/woman	the Irish
America	=	American	the Americans

	Eggs	Milk *litres*	Fish *kilos*	Beer *pints*	Fruit *kilos*
Britain	236	111		190	
France		44	7		83
Italy	206			4	
Russia		95	8.5		51
Australia	198			206	
Japan		31	41		38
Ireland	240			178	
America		113	8		70

3 *Talk about the countries with your friend.*

► *eg* The French drink more milk than the Japanese but less than the British.
The Irish drink the most milk and the Japanese the least.

4 *Use information from the chart and compare three countries.*

Unit 19a I'll be in Denmark

1 *Write these future times in the chart in the correct order.*

next Saturday
next April
next summer
at 8 o'clock next Sunday
next Friday week
next Christmas Day
on your next birthday
in five minutes time
next Monday morning

Times	You	Your friend

2 *Alan and his parents want to invite Derek to dinner. Listen and answer these questions.*

a. Will Derek go to dinner at Alan's house next Saturday?
b. Why not?
c. Will Derek have dinner with Alan next Saturday week?

3 *Listen and repeat.*

Where will you be?
I'll be in Denmark.
I won't be in England.
Will you be in England?
Yes, I will.
No, I won't.
I'll return to London on Thursday.

4 *Look at the chart in Exercise 1. Write where you will be at the various times. Then ask a friend where he or she will be at those times.*

► *eg* A: Will you be in this classroom in five minutes time?
B: No, I won't.
A: Where will you be in five minutes time?
B: I'll be in the playground.

5 *Ask your friend these questions about the times in the pictures.*

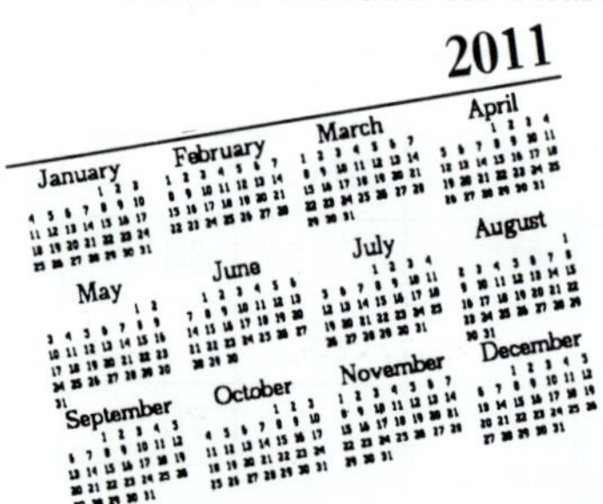

Where / How / When — will you — go? / travel? / be? / return?

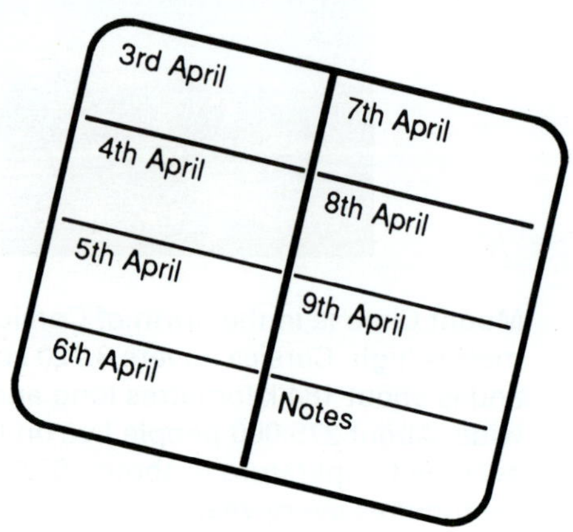

Unit 19b When I'm twenty-five

1 *Look at the questionnaire and tick (√) for **yes**.*

When I'm twenty-five I . . .

☐ will be rich	☐ will be poor
☐ will be famous	☐ won't be famous
☐ will drive a car	☐ won't drive a car
☐ will be married	☐ won't be married
☐ will have children	☐ won't have children
☐ will live in my country	☐ will live abroad
☐ will live in a house	☐ will live in a flat
☐ will have a pet	☐ won't have a pet
☐ will speak English well	☐ won't speak English well

2 *Listen and repeat.*

Will you be rich when you're twenty-five?
Yes, I will.
No, I won't.

3 *With a friend ask and answer. Use the questionnaire.*

► *eg* A: Will you be rich when you're twenty-five?
B: Yes, I will./No, I won't.

4 *Beatrix is thinking about her future. Read and answer the questions.*

a. Will she live in Holland?
b. Will she speak a lot of languages?
c. Will she be married when she's twenty-five?
d. Will she be rich?
e. Will she travel a lot?

When I'm twenty-five I'll live in a big house in a hot country. I won't live in a cold country because I love the sun. I'll have a fantastic job and I'll have lots of money. I'll be a famous pop singer and I'll travel all over the world. I'll speak a lot of languages. I won't be married – I'll get married when I'm thirty.

5 *Write some questions to ask your friend about when he or she is twenty-five. Then ask your friend the questions and note the answers.*

6 *Write a paragraph about your friend when he or she is twenty-five. Begin:*

When ______ is twenty-five years old he'll/she'll be rich, he/she won't be poor . . . .

Unit 19c Will it rain in Birmingham?

1 *Write sentences about the pictures. Use these words:*

cloudy cold foggy hot rain snow sunny windy ► *eg* It'll be sunny.

a. b. c. d. e. f. g. h.

2 *Listen and repeat.*

Will it rain in Birmingham tomorrow?
Yes, it will.
No, it won't.
What will the weather be like in Manchester tomorrow?
It'll be sunny.

3 *Look at the weather forecast for Britain tomorrow. Ask and answer.*

► *eg* A: What will the weather be like in Manchester tomorrow?
B: It'll be sunny.
A: Will it be sunny in London?
B: No, it won't.

4 *Listen and look at the map of Europe. Tick (√) the correct symbols and cross (×) the wrong symbols.*

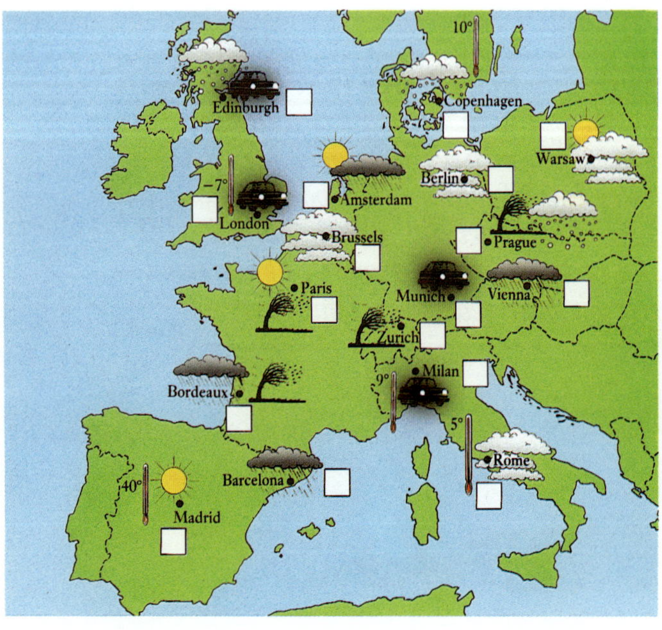

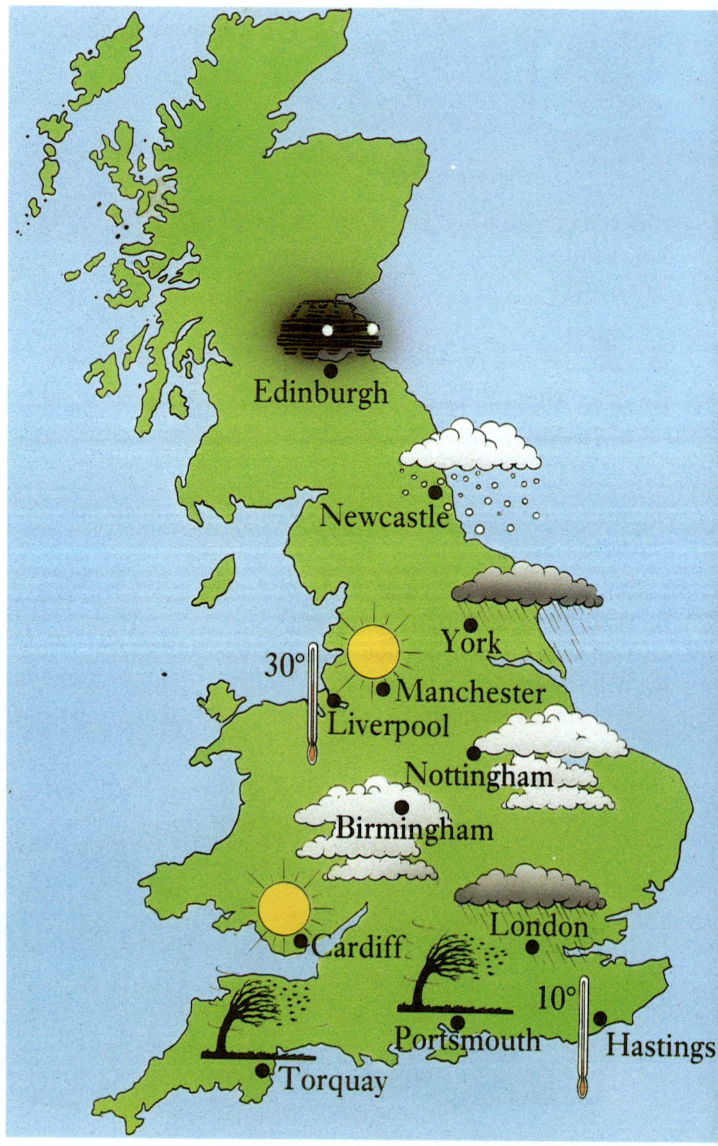

future form: *will* p 110 /aʊ/ **cloud**

Unit 19d You'll go to the mountains . . .

1 *Find and read your Colour Quarter Holiday Horoscope. Then answer these questions.*

a. Where will you go for your holidays?
b. What will the weather be like?
c. What will you do during the day?

2 *Find a friend with a different Colour Quarter. Ask and answer about where, weather and what (during day).*

Colour Quarter Holiday Horoscopes

5

What the stars say will happen to you this summer

Blue Quarter
January, February, March

You'll go to a hot country and you'll play on the beach every day. You'll make a lot of new friends. You'll take part in a lot of sports competitions but you won't win anything. The weather will get colder at the end of your holiday and you'll be happy to return home.

Red Quarter
April, May, June

You'll go to the beach for your holiday but you'll arrive late. You'll have some problems with your school examinations. You'll study history and maths during your holiday. You'll be ill for a week in the middle of your holiday. The weather will be very hot at the beginning and at the end. It will rain a lot for a few days in the middle of your holiday.

Green Quarter
July, August, September

You'll go to the mountains for your holiday. The weather will be sunny and hot. You'll go for long walks in the mountains and meet some old friends. You'll go for picnics and play sports in the afternoons. You won't study during your stay in the mountains because your examination results will be very good.

Yellow Quarter
October, November, December

You'll go to the country for your next holidays. It'll rain for the first week and then the weather will get better. The last week will be very sunny and hot. You'll go to the market every morning and you'll play cards with your friends in the afternoons.

Unit 19 — Chatterbox A

Chatterbox B see page *102*.

Next Saturday Derek will go to Copenhagen, in Denmark, to see the Teen Eye agent and Karin.

1 *Ask your friend questions and fill in the chart.*

► *eg* A: What time will he get up on Sunday?
B: He'll get up at half past seven.
A: What will he do at eight o'clock on Saturday?
B: He'll arrive at the airport.

2 *Answer your friend's questions.*

Saturday		Sunday	
7.00	leave home	....	get up
8.00	....	8.30	....
9.30	plane takes off	....	drive to Open Air Museum
11.00	....	9.30	visit museum
12.00	arrive air terminal	....	return to Copenhagen
12.30	....	2.00	take photographs of city
2.00	phone Fatma in London	....	say goodbye to Karin
2.30	....	5.30	get bus to airport
3.30	leave agent's office	6.30	bus arrives at airport
4.00	....	8.00	....
5.30	visit Tivoli Gardens	10.30	plane lands at Heathrow Airport
		12.00	....

Unit 20 Language check

Teen Eye on food and drink

1 *Match the pictures and the descriptions.*

1. something made with two pieces of bread with cold food between them
2. something made with milk
3. something made with the leaf of a plant
4. something made from a fruit
5. a special container for cooking quickly
6. something made from a secret formula
7. a breakfast cereal
8. a method of keeping food for a long time
9. something made from red vegetables
10. a special container for liquids
11. something made from the bean of a plant
12. a special machine for keeping food cold

a.☐ b.☐ c.☐ d.☐ e.☐ f.☐ g.☐ h.☐ i.☐ j.☐ k.☐ l.☐

2 *Listen to Jane and Derek and fill in the missing dates and products.*

dates	products	countries/ nationalities
.... BC	....	Asia
....	tea	....
2000 BC	....	Crete
....	....	Ethiopia
....	....	....
....	....	England
....	fridge	French
		inventors
....	tomato ketchup	Henry ....
....	Coca Cola	John Pemberton
....	....	Keith ....
....	frozen food	Clarence ....
....	Tetra Pak containers	
1994	.... sold in .... countries	

3 *Listen again and fill in the missing information about the countries/nationalities and inventors.*

4 *Use your notes and write a paragraph about the history of food and drink.*

5 *In pairs choose food or drinks or machines and write sentences describing them. Use the descriptions in Exercise 1 to help you. Then work in small groups and say your sentences. The other students must guess the object.*

6 *Read and answer the questions.*

What will the world be like in 2050? Fifty young people met and discussed the question. Some of the answers were very interesting.

Some of the young people say that cities will be bigger but more beautiful, with lots of parks and trees. Some of them think that there will be fewer people in Europe, so cities will be smaller. There will be more farms and they will grow food for all the world and we will give, not sell, food to the poorer people.

Athletes will be stronger and faster in 2050 – someone will run 1,500 metres in two and a half minutes! The world's tallest man will be 2.90 metres tall. Most young people think that men will be between 1.75 and 2.00 metres tall in the year 2050. They also think that women will be as tall as men. Men and women will wear the same clothes but in different colours. No-one will go to school. Students will learn at home with a computer. The computers will be joined to a computer in the teacher's house. Each computer will have a two-way television screen so students can see and hear the teacher and the other students. The computer will also correct the homework for the students!

At weekends, people will go to the Moon and have a picnic there. Maybe they will go to a museum. Museums will be more interesting because they will have things from other planets, too. Tennis competitions on Venus, Mercury and the Moon will be very popular. They will be very different because there is a different atmosphere on the planets. Back on Earth, people will sleep on anti-gravity beds. Sweet dreams!

a. What will bigger cities look like in the year 2050?
b. Why do some of the young people think that cities will be smaller?
c. Where will the poor countries get food from?
d. Who will run 1,500 metres in two and a half minutes?
e. How will people change in the year 2050?
f. How tall will women be?
g. How will women's clothes be different from men's clothes?
h. Who will go to school?
i. How will students study?
j. How will students talk to the teacher?
k. What will people do at the weekend?
l. Why will people go to museums?
m. Why will tennis be popular?
n. Where will people sleep?

7 *In groups, find out what your friends think the world will be like in the year 2050. Ask about:*

cities food sports men and women
clothes school free time space

8 *Write about what your friends think the world will be like in the year 2050. Use the text in Exercise 6 as a model.*

Unit 21a I went there to see my friend

1 *Derek's having dinner with Alan and his family. Listen and answer.*

a. Did Derek like Denmark?
b. Why did he visit Aarhus?
c. Why did he go to Odense?
d. Why did Mrs Bailey go to Denmark?
e. Where did she stay?
f. Did she like Denmark?

2 *Listen and repeat.*

Why did you go there?
I went to Odense to have a short holiday.
I went there to stay with my pen-friend.

3 *Make a list of five towns or places you visited last year. Give the list to a friend. Then ask and answer.*

▶ *eg* A: Why did you go to Rome?
B: I went to Rome to see the Colosseum.

4 *Read.*

How?	Where?	Why?
He walked	to the shops	to buy some apples.

5 *Make a list of eight places you went to last month.*

▶ *eg* cinema

Then add how you got to these places.

▶ *eg* by bus

Now write why you went to these places.

▶ *eg* to see new Batman film.

6 *In pairs or small groups ask and answer. Make notes of your friends' answers.*

Where did you go?
How did you get there?
Why did you go there?

7 *Use your notes and write sentences.*

infinitive of purpose: *to* + verb p 100 /aɪ/ why

Unit 21b I was doing my homework

1 *Derek is talking to Jane. Listen and choose the right picture.*

2 *Listen and repeat.*

Who was the first person you saw this morning?
What were you doing when you saw her?
While you were walking into the kitchen, your mother was standing on her head.

3 *Listen and read. Then practise the dialogue with a friend.*

A: Who was the second teacher you saw this morning?
B: Mr Alison.
A: What was he doing when you saw him?
B: He was coming into the classroom.
A: What were you doing when you saw him?
B: While he was coming into the classroom, I was finishing my homework!

4 *Make changes to the dialogue. Then practise with a friend. Start with these ideas:*

first	person	this morning
second	student	after lunch today
	teacher	at school this morning

5 *Write one of the dialogues.*

Unit 21c Loch Ness

1 *Find out:*

a. Where Loch Ness is.
b. Why it is famous.

2 *Do you have similar stories or places in your country?*

3 *Look at the pictures. Describe one of them. Your friend must guess which picture.*

4 *Derek and Fatma are talking about what happened to Derek at Loch Ness in Scotland this morning. Listen to Derek and Fatma. Then number the pictures in the right order.*

5 *Listen again and make notes about each picture.*

6 *Listen and repeat*

While I was changing the film, I dropped the video camera. And while I was picking up the camera, the new film fell out of it.

7 *Use your notes and write the story. Begin:*

Last week Derek was filming at Loch Ness . . .

b. ☐

a. ☐

c. ☐

d. ☐

e. ☐

f. ☐

interrupted past continuous tense p 110

/eə/ where

Unit 21d Who saw the monster?

After all the problems Derek had with his camera at Loch Ness, he returned to the loch in the afternoon with Fatma and Jane.

1 *Look at the picture and read the text. Some of the information in the text is not correct. Find the sentences that are not correct.*

The afternoon at Loch Ness

At four o'clock Derek, Fatma and Jane all returned to Loch Ness by train. They started filming at five and at half past five the monster appeared in the loch. It was swimming away from the Teen Eye team. They didn't see the monster because Derek was talking to Jane near a big tree and Fatma was writing some notes. An old man was walking beside the loch. He saw the monster. He was carrying a walking stick and he threw it at the monster.

2 *Write the sentences so that they describe the picture.*

► *eg* They didn't return to Loch Ness by train, they returned by van.

Unit 21 **Chatterbox A**

Chatterbox B see page *102*.

Last Friday was a terrible day for Pedro because everything broke!

1 *Ask your friend questions about the missing pictures. Write sentences.*

► *eg* A: What happened while Pedro was brushing his teeth?
B: While Pedro was brushing his teeth his toothbrush broke.
A: What was Pedro doing when his toothbrush broke?
B: When his toothbrush broke he was brushing his teeth.

These words will help you:

1. brush 2. tie shoelaces 3. satchel strap
4. open door 5. lift 6. cycle to school

2 *Answer your friend's questions.*

1. 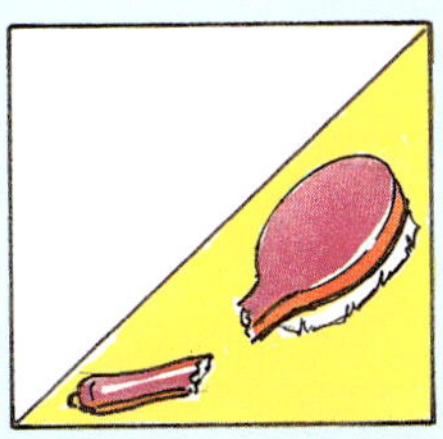
2. 
3. 
4. 
5. 

6. 

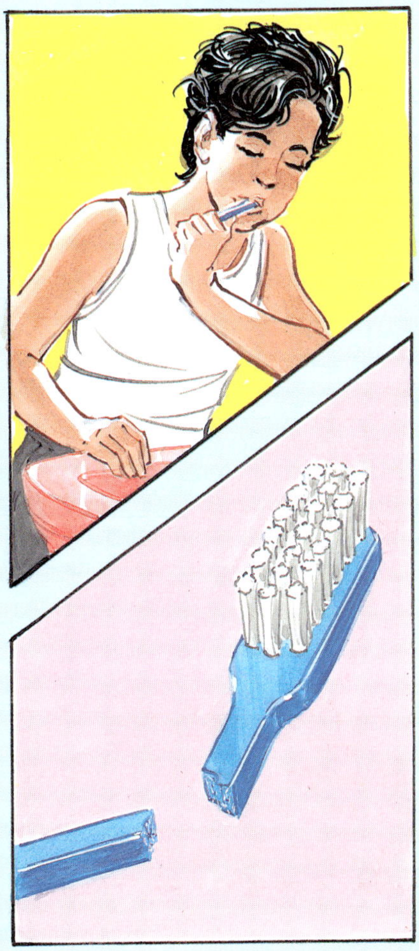

Unit 22a Have you ever played chess?

1 *Find these words in the picture.*

☐ ankle ☐ arm ☐ finger ☐ leg
☐ nose ☐ shoulder ☐ toe ☐ wrist

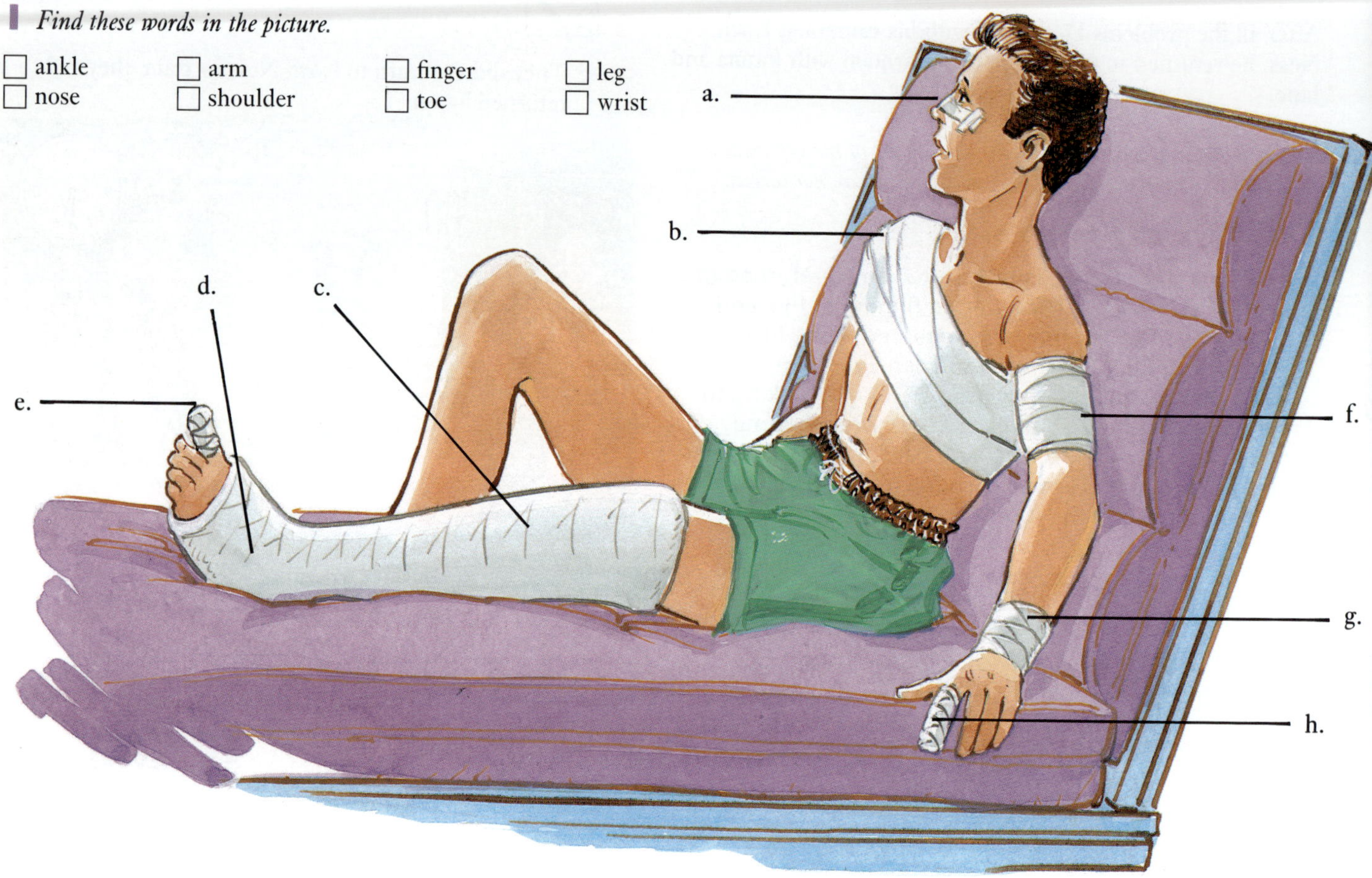

2 *Pedro wants to join a Sports Centre in London. He is talking to the Medical Officer of the Centre. Listen and tick (√)* ***True*** *or* ***False****. Correct the false statements.*

	True	False
a. Pedro plays a lot of cricket.	☐	☐
b. Pedro has got a broken arm.	☐	☐
c. Pedro's mother isn't in Portugal.	☐	☐
d. Pedro will phone his mother.	☐	☐
e. The Medical Officer will phone Pedro's mother.	☐	☐

3 *Listen and repeat.*

Have you ever broken your arm?
Yes, I have.
No, I haven't.
I don't remember.

4 *Look at the picture in Exercise 1. Ask and answer.*

► *eg* A: Have you ever broken your ankle?
B: Yes, I have./No, I haven't./I don't remember.

5 *In groups make a list of all the sports you know. Find out how many students in your class have played the sports.*

► *eg* A: Have you ever played baseball?
B: Yes, I have./No, I haven't.

present perfect tense + *ever* p 110 /æ/ **ankle** /ɑ:/ **arm**

Unit 22b Has he ever had measles?

a. ☐

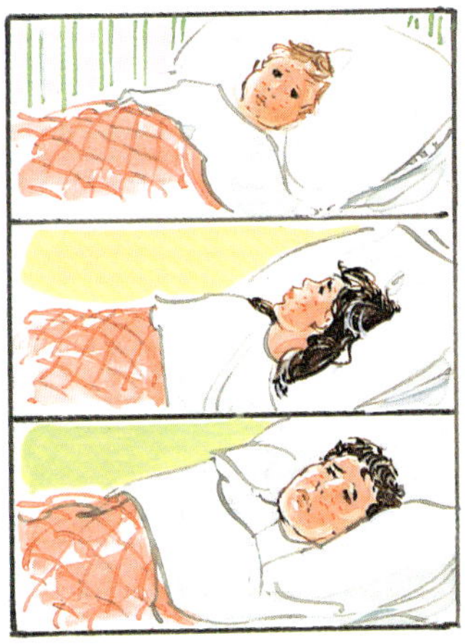

b. ☐

c. ☐

d. ☐

1 *Match the illnesses and the anagrams. Then match the illnesses and the pictures.*

1. chicken pox	clerats refve
2. whooping cough	easmsel
3. scarlet fever	brualle
4. mumps	nicheck xpo
5. rubella	smupm
6. measles	howignpo hugoc

2 *In column A, tick (√) the illnesses you have had.*

A	Illness	B
	chicken pox	
	measles	✓
	mumps	
	whooping cough	
	rubella	
	scarlet fever	

3 *Listen to the Medical Officer and Pedro's mother. In column B, tick the illnesses Pedro has had.*

4 *Listen and repeat.*

Has he ever had measles?
Yes, he has.
Has he ever had mumps?
No, he hasn't.

5 *Ask your friend about the illnesses in Exercise 2. Write the answers.*

▶ *eg* A: Have you ever had chicken pox?
B: Yes, I have./No, I haven't.

6 *Ask and answer with another friend.*

▶ *eg* A: Has David ever had chicken pox?
B: Yes, he has./No, he hasn't.

7 *Write sentences about your friend's partner.*

▶ *eg* David has never had mumps but he has had measles.

What is a strawberry?
It's a cherry with measles!

present perfect tense + *ever* p 110 /f/ cough

Unit 22c Have you ever won a medal?

1 *Look at these verbs. Write the correct form of each verb in the chart.*

Verb	Past	Past participle
lose	lost	lost
break	....	....
have	....	....
win	....	....
play	....	....
be	....	....
cut	....	....
see	....	....

2 *Write the verbs in the questionnaire. Use each verb twice. Then ask your friends questions. You must not ask the same person more than two questions.*

When the answer is 'yes' write the name of your friend in the chart.

► *eg* A: Have you ever lost your exercise book?
B: Yes, I have./No, I haven't.

3 *Read these answers carefully. Then listen to the questions. Write the question numbers next to their answers.*

Question number	Answers
☐	a. Yes, I have. I've left it on the bus six times this term.
☐	b. Yes, he has – when he was helping his mother in the kitchen.
☐	c. No, I haven't. It's too difficult to eat.
☐	d. Yes, I have. I was in bed for two weeks.
☐	e. Yes, I have. I've seen one at the circus.
☐	f. No, I haven't. I don't like swimming.
☐	g. Yes, he has – when he went skiing last year.
☐	h. Yes, she went last year.
☐	i. Yes, she had it when she was a child.
☐	j. Yes, I have. I met Tom Cruise in a restaurant.

Class questionnaire

	verb		friend's name
a.	....	exercise book	....
b.	....	leg	....
c.	....	elephant	....
d.	....	England	....
e.	....	measles	....
f.	....	snake	....
g.	....	medal	....
h.	....	cricket	....
i.	....	nose	....
j.	....	watch	....
k.	....	circus	....
l.	....	cards	....
m.	....	race	....
n.	....	mumps	....
o.	....	finger	....

present perfect tense + *ever* p 110 /eɪ/ **play** /ɪ/ **win** /iː/ **be**

Unit 22d World class

1 *Read about Mark Hawkins and answer the questions.*

a. What sport is Mark good at?
b. Why did he miss the Olympics?

World Class

Mark Hawkins is a world champion skiier. But his life hasn't been easy. He has broken every bone in his body except for his right arm. In fact he's broken his left leg four times, the last time during training!

He's travelled all over the world and he's won every major competition except for the Olympic Games. He missed the last Winter Games because he had measles.

In his sporting life he's lost only ten competitions. Now he's waiting for the next Olympic Games. He wants to win a medal there. Then he will stop skiing.

2 *Read again and tick (√)* ***True*** *or* ***False****. Correct the false statements.*

	True	False
a. Mark's life has been easy.	☐	☐
b. He's broken his right arm.	☐	☐
c. He's broken his nose.	☐	☐
d. He's broken his left leg three times.	☐	☐
e. He's been to many countries in the world.	☐	☐
f. He's won every major competition.	☐	☐
g. He's had measles.	☐	☐
h. He's won only ten competitions.	☐	☐

Unit 22 — *Chatterbox A*

Chatterbox B see page *103*.

1 *Listen to the dialogues in Unit 22a and Unit 22b again and tick (√) or cross (×) the information about Pedro.*

2 *Ask your friend about Eric and fill in the chart.*

► *eg* A: Has Eric ever broken his leg?
B: Yes, he has./No, he hasn't.

3 *Answer your friend's questions about Paul.*

4 *Write sentences about Pedro.*

► *eg* He's never broken his arm, but he's broken his leg.

	Pedro	Eric	Paul		Pedro	Eric	Paul
Broken: leg			×	**Illness:** scarlet fever			×
finger			√	rubella			√
arm			√	whooping cough			√
ankle			×	mumps			√
nose			×	chicken pox			√
toe			√	measles			√

Unit 23a Have you seen it yet?

1 *Match the actors and actresses to the films they star in. Then tick (√) the films you have seen.*

a. ☐ Alien

b. ☐ Superman

c. ☐ Indiana Jones

d. ☐ The Mask

e. ☐ Jurassic Park

f. ☐ Batman

g. ☐ Back to the Future

h. ☐ Star Wars

1. Michael J Fox
2. Jim Carrey
3. Christopher Reeve
4. Laura Dern
5. Harrison Ford
6. Sigourney Weaver
7. Michelle Pfeiffer
8. Carrie Fisher

2 *Alan, Mikis and Karin want to go to the cinema. They are reading a newspaper and talking about films. Listen and tick (√) the films Alan, Mikis and Karin have seen.*

	Batman	Superman	Alien
Alan			
Mikis			
Karin			

3 *Listen and repeat.*

Have you seen the new *Batman* film yet?
Yes, I have.
I've already seen it.
Have you seen the new *Alien* film yet?
No, I haven't.

4 *Look at the films in Exercise 1. Ask and answer.*

► *eg* A: Have you seen the new *Alien* film yet?
B: Yes, I have./No, I haven't.

5 *Listen and read. Then practise the dialogue with a friend.*

Alan: Mum! Can I go to the cinema with my friends?
Mrs Bailey: Yes, OK. Don't be home late!
Alan: No, Mum. Bye.
Mrs Bailey: Wait a minute! Have you *done* your *homework* yet?
Alan: *Done* my *homework*! Of course I have.
Mrs Bailey: Hmm. OK. Bye.

6 *Make changes to the dialogue and practise with a friend. Use these words:*

do/homework clean/bedroom put away/records
take/dog for a walk practise/piano have/dinner

present perfect tense + *yet/already* p 110 /j/ **yet**

Unit 23b I've been here for hours!

1 *Divide these times into two lists. What is the difference between the two lists?*

yesterday two weeks 1st April last night a long time
a month Christmas 10 minutes about two years
three days the weekend Thursday

yesterday......	two weeks......
....	....
....	....
....	....
....	....
....	....

2 *Karin is at the Teen Eye studio in Brussels. Suddenly her grandmother walks in the door. Listen and answer these questions.*

a. Where has Karin's grandmother been?
b. Where is she going tomorrow?

3 *Listen again and number the pictures in the right order.*

a. ☐ b. ☐

c. ☐

d. ☐

4 *Listen and repeat.*

How long have you been here?
I've been in Belgium for about five hours.
I haven't seen you since Christmas.

5 *Read.*

I've studied English **for two years**.
She's studied English **since 1989**.
We've been here **for three hours**.
They've been there **since five o'clock**.

6 *Ask a friend about these places and note the answers.*

this town this school this class the classroom your house

▶ *eg* A: How long have you lived in this town?
B: I've lived in this town since 1987.

7 *Ask another friend about his or her partner.*

▶ *eg* A: How long has she lived in this town?
B: She's lived in this town for thirteen years.

Unit 23c The classical guitar

1 *Have you ever played a guitar? When did you play it?*

2 *Match the names and the parts of the guitar.*

☐ neck ☐ soundbox ☐ bridge ☐ strings

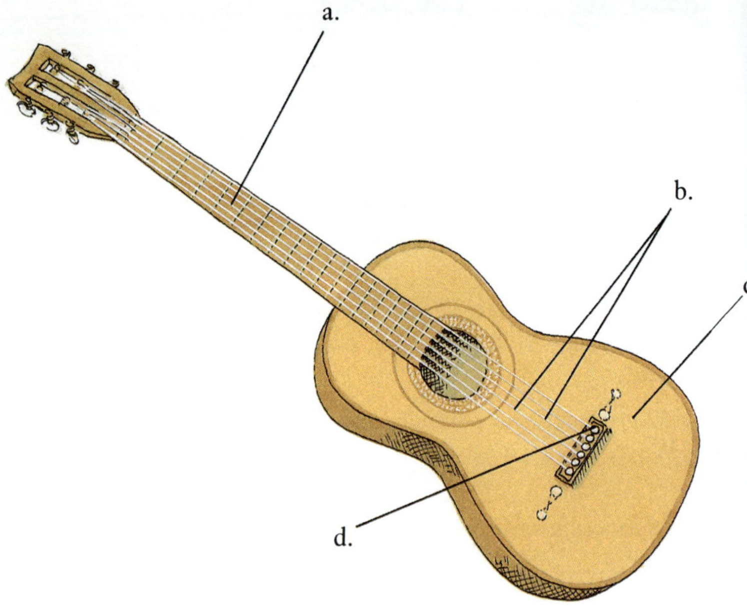

3 *Read.*

Which country has been the centre of the development of the classical guitar?

Since the twelfth century, one country has been the centre of development of the classical guitar. Six or seven great men, most of them Spanish, have developed the guitar we know today. Fernando Sor (1778–1839) composed over four hundred pieces of music for the guitar. He travelled and met famous guitar makers, called *luthiers*, in France and London. They loved Sor's Spanish guitar and started making their guitars in the same way. These guitars became famous all over the world.

Another Spaniard, Antonio de Torres Juardo (1817–1892) made the next big change. When musicians played one of his guitars, they threw away their old guitars because the sound of the new guitar was so beautiful.

The design of classical guitars hasn't changed since Torres made his changes. He increased the size of the soundbox and reduced the thickness of the wood. He also used new varnishes on the wood to improve the sound. With these improvements in the guitar it was possible to play classical music. Another Spaniard, Francisco Eixea Tarrega (1852–1909), the father of all modern guitar techniques, re-wrote the music of Bach, Beethoven and Mozart for the guitar. He also developed the hand positions, the way to hold a guitar, and the use of a footstool to improve guitar playing. The brilliant Andres Segovia (1893–1987), more than any other man, made the classical guitar famous the world over.

4 *Read the text again and answer.*

a. What are *luthiers*?
b. Where did Sor meet *luthiers*?
c. Why did people throw away their guitars after playing a Torres guitar?
d. How was Torres' guitar different?
e. Why is Tarrega famous?
f. Who was Segovia?

5 *Use the answers to Exercise 4 to write the story of the Spanish classical guitar. Join the sentences with these words:*

and   and so   when   because

present perfect tense p 110 /k/ **c**ountry

Unit 23d Past and future

1 The young people in the Teen Eye team change every year. This year's group are all meeting in London for the last time. Listen and make notes about what Beatrix and Alan have done during the year and what they are going to do in the future.

2 *Compare your notes with your friend.*

3 *Listen again and write as much detail as possible.*

4 *Use your notes from Exercise 1 and practise the dialogue with a friend.*

What have they done?		What are they going to do?	
Alan	Beatrix	Alan	Beatrix

Unit 23 Chatterbox A

Chatterbox B see page *103*.

How long has everybody been at the Teen Eye office today?

1 *Read the text. Fill in as much of the chart as you can.*

2 *Ask your friend questions and fill in the rest of the chart.*

▶ *eg* A: Who arrived at half past eight?
B: Bill did.

Note: *Sometimes more than one person arrived at the same time.*

3 *Write two sentences each about Beatrix, Karin, Alan, Mikis, Fatma, Françoise, Pedro, Jane and Derek.*

▶ *eg* Bill has been at the office since half past eight.
Bill has been at the office for three and a half hours.

Bill, the doorman at the Teen Eye offices, was the first to arrive this morning. He arrived at half past eight. Derek arrived at nine o'clock and Fatma arrived half an hour after Jane. Alan entered Teen Eye half an hour before Françoise but half an hour after Pedro. The time is now twelve o'clock.

Time	Name(s)
8.30	
9.00	
9.30	
10.00	
10.30	
11.00	
11.30	

Unit 24a Has she been here recently?

1 *Write a verb next to the words. Use each of these verbs twice:*

go eat buy play clean

Where	Yes/No	When
play../tennis		
........./shoes		
........./Italian food		
........./new coat		
........./room		
........./Chinese food		
........./cinema		
........./football		
........./new pair of shoes		
........./theatre		

2 *Jane has been in hospital for a few months. Today is her first day at work for a long time. She is in the studio talking to Derek. Listen and answer the questions.*

a. Is Beatrix in England now?
b. Is Karin in England now?
c. Why does Jane want to see Karin?
d. What kind of party are they going to have?
e. When did Fatma finish the Olympics programme?
f. What is Jane going to do this week?

3 *Listen and repeat.*

Have you seen her recently?
No, I haven't.
Has she finished the programme?
Yes, she has.
When did she finish it?
Two weeks ago.

4 *Ask and answer about the places and activities in Exercise 1 and fill in the chart.*

► *eg* A: Have you played tennis recently?
B: Yes, I have.
A: When did you play?
B: I played last week.
A: Have you bought new shoes recently?
B: No, I haven't.

5 *Write complete sentences about your friend.*

► *eg* David played tennis last week but he hasn't played football recently.

6 *Make a list of six things you have done recently. Ask your friend if he or she has done these things. If the answer is yes, ask when your friend did them.*

present perfect tense + *recently*/past simple tense + *ago* p 110 unstressed have /həv/ stressed haven't /ˈhævnt/

Unit 24 b She's just gone home

1 *Fatma is telephoning Derek. She is very worried. Listen and tick (√) the correct answers.*

a. Peter Brown telephoned

A a few minutes ago ☐ **B** an hour ago ☐

b. Derek made the appointment with the dentist

A last week ☐ **B** very recently ☐

c. Jane went home

A half an hour ago ☐ **B** a short time ago ☐

2 *Listen and repeat.*

I've just made an appointment.
She's just gone home.

3 *Look at the pictures and complete the sentences.*

a. .... sent a parcel.
b. A man has just posted ....
c. A woman has .... some stamps.
d. .... bought some aerogrammes.

4 *Look at the pictures and complete the sentences.*

a. Fatma .... letter.
b. Derek has just come into ....
c. Jane has .... made some ....
d. Fatma .... glasses.
e. Derek .... off .... coat.
f. Jane .... answered ....

5 *Read the sentences. Then put them in the correct order in the dialogues. Practise the dialogues.*

a. It was all right.
Superman III.
What film did you see?
Hi, where have you been?
Did you like it?
I've been to the cinema.

b. Where was she?
Have you seen Karin?
She was studying in the library.
Yes, I have.

6 *In pairs make a list of six things you've just done. Change partners and find out if your new partner has just done the things on your list.*

▶ *eg* Have you just closed your schoolbag?

Unit 24c Where are you going to stay?

1 *Answer the questions.*

a. When are you going on your next summer holiday?
b. Where are you going?
c. Are you going to the beach or to the mountains?
d. Who are you going with?
e. How are you going to travel?
f. Where are you going to stay?

2 *Fatma, Mikis and Karin are talking about their next holidays. Listen and fill in the chart.*

Name	Where go?	Where stay?			How long?		
		hotel	campsite	family	1 week	2 weeks	3 weeks
Fatma							
Mikis							
Karin							

3 *Use the information in the chart and write the conversation in your own words.*

4 *Ask your friends about their next holidays. Make notes of their answers.*

5 *Write a paragraph about your friend's next holiday.*

future form: *going to* p 106

/w/ **when** /h/ **how**

Unit 24d Time for a bath!

1 *Read the story and number the pictures in the right order.*

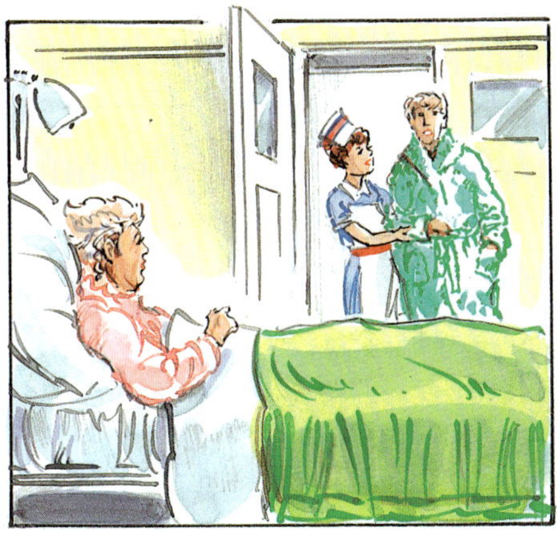

a. ☐

b. ☐

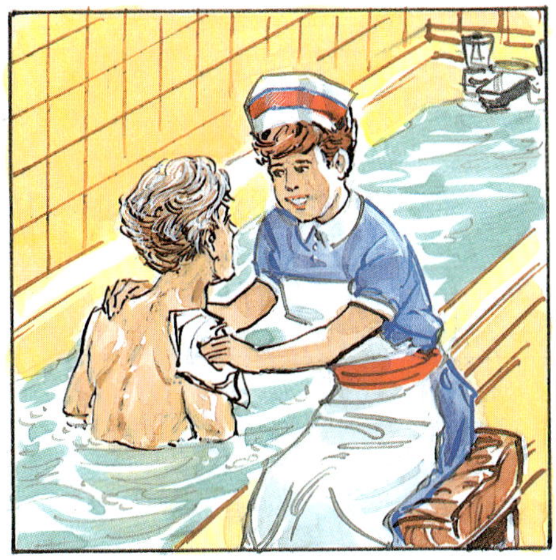

c. ☐

Nurses in hospitals in England are very good at their jobs. Student nurses work in hospitals for a long time before they become nurses.

One day last October, in a London hospital, the head nurse sent a very enthusiastic student nurse to one of the wards for old people. It was time to bath the patients.

There was an old lady sitting on the first bed. 'Time for your bath,' said the student nurse.
'I've already had one today, thank you very much,' said the old lady.
'Poor old lady,' thought the nurse. 'She's a bit crazy.'

The nurse took the old lady to the bathroom, took off all her clothes and gave her a bath. They went back to the ward together. The nurse was very surprised. 'Look! There's another old lady in your bed,' she said.

'It's my sister,' said the very clean old lady. 'I've come to visit her!'

2 *Ask and answer these questions with a friend.*

a. Where does the story take place?
b. How many people are in the story?
c. Did the old lady want a bath?
d. Did the student nurse give a bath to the right person?
e. Why did she make a mistake?
f. When did the nurse realise her mistake?

3 *Write the dialogue between the old lady and her sister after the student nurse left.*

Unit 24 *Chatterbox A*

Chatterbox B see page *104*.

1 *Ask your friend questions about Alan and fill in the chart.*

▶ *eg* A: Has Alan been to the zoo recently?
B: Yes, he has. He's been there this month.
A: Has he eaten Spanish food recently?
B: No, he hasn't. He ate some over a year ago.

2 *Answer your friend's questions.*

Activity	over two years ago	over a year ago	this month	this week
go/zoo			✓	
eat/Spanish food		✓		
play/basketball	✓			
buy/new satchel			✓	
go/seaside				
visit/relations				
eat/Greek food		✓		
play/handball				
visit/sick friend				✓
buy/new bicycle				
go/Brussels			✓	
eat/French bread				

Unit 25 Language check

Teen Eye on the Olympic Games

1 *Describe one of the pictures. Your friend must guess which one.*

2 *Read about the Olympic Games and match the paragraphs and the pictures. Then put the paragraphs in order.*

A Coroelus of Elis has just won the first race in the first Olympic Games. The people give Coroelus a crown of wild olives, and later they will build a statue of him.

B All the different kinds of skiing are now in separate Games, the Winter Olympics. These games have happened every four years since 1924. Any sport that people play in at least twenty-five countries can become an Olympic sport.

C In 1896, the Olympic Games started again. A Frenchman, Baron Pierre de Coubertin, organised the first modern Olympic Games in Athens, Greece. The most important rule for athletes in the Games was: 'All athletes must be amateurs and not receive money for taking part in competitions.' In recent years, this rule has been changed so that professionals can take part, especially in team sports such as football and basketball.

D The modern Olympics take place every four years in different countries. The Games bring together the best young sportsmen and sportswomen. They participate not for crowns of wild olives or statues but for the joy and happiness of taking part in the Games – and, of course, for the medals.

E The year is 776 BC, the place is Olympia in Greece. On a summer's day, forty thousand people are watching a race. Twenty men are running along a valley. A young man, dressed in white, is the first person to reach the end of the valley. Everybody jumps up, shouting for joy.

F The Games celebrated pagan gods, especially Zeus. When Christianity became popular, the Games became unpopular. Eventually, in AD 393, nearly 1,300 years after the first Olympics, a Christian Emperor stopped the Games.

a. ☐

b. ☐

c. ☐

d. ☐

e. ☐

f. ☐

3 *Read the story again and find words which mean:*

a. pleasure .... b. not together ....
c. take part ....

4 *Cover the story and look at the pictures. Tell the story to your friend.*

Unit 25

5 *How European are you? Answer the questions and find out.*

The Europe Quiz

1. When was the Treaty of Rome, which started the European Community, signed?

   1945 ☐ 1957 ☐ 1973 ☐

2. How many countries signed the Treaty of Rome?

   12 ☐ 8 ☐ 6 ☐

3. Which is the largest country in the EC?

   Germany ☐ France ☐ Greece ☐

4. Which is the smallest country in the EC?

   Luxembourg ☐ Holland ☐ Ireland ☐

5. What are the capital cities of the fifteen EC countries?

Austria	....	France	....	Italy	....
Belgium	....	Germany	....	Luxembourg	....
Britain	....	Greece	....	Portugal	....
Denmark	....	Holland	....	Spain	....
Finland	....	Ireland	....	Sweden	....

6. Match the countries and the languages. Some countries have more than one language.

Luxembourg	German
France	Gaelic
Belgium	French
The Netherlands	English
Ireland	Dutch
England	Flemish
Germany	
Austria	

7. Which European countries are famous for these foods and drinks?

a. paella	....	f. Frankfurter sausages	....
b. Edam cheese	....	g. Guinness	....
c. roast beef	....	h. pizza	....
d. Beaujolais wine	....	i. sardines	....
e. moussaka	....	j. sangria	....

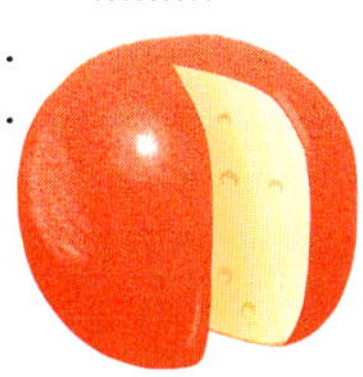

8. Find the European nationalities.

Austrian	Irish
British	Italian
Danish	~~Polish~~
French	Portuguese
German	Spanish
Greek	Turkish

P	E	R	K	S	I	R	T	N	T	N	H	A
D	O	B	K	A	U	E	N	U	A	A	J	H
R	F	R	E	N	C	H	H	M	T	I	H	S
E	R	I	T	G	L	O	R	S	F	L	G	I
D	S	T	U	U	T	E	W	P	H	A	F	L
X	G	I	D	S	G	I	O	A	S	T	D	O
L	O	S	H	R	S	U	H	N	D	I	D	P
N	O	H	E	S	D	S	E	I	L	R	O	R
S	D	E	N	A	I	R	T	S	U	A	K	E
A	K	H	S	K	F	N	G	H	E	S	A	O
L	I	I	R	I	S	H	A	H	E	O	O	P
A	A	U	H	E	I	R	T	D	L	E	J	N
A	T	F	U	T	I	R	U	E	M	D	L	E

Chatterbox B

Unit 1

Chatterbox B

Chatterbox A see page *6*.

1 *Ask your friend questions about Jane and fill in the form.*

2 *Answer your friend's questions about Derek.*

First name	....	**First name**	Derek
Surname	....	**Surname**	Farley
Age	....	**Age**	28
Nationality	....	**Nationality**	English
Country	....	**Country**	England
City	....	**City**	Southampton
Favourite hobby	....	**Favourite hobby**	Taking photographs

Unit 2

Chatterbox B

Chatterbox A see page *10*.

1 *Look at the map. Ask your friend how to get to these places:*

football stadium doctor's bank
his/her house park record shop

► *eg* B: Excuse me. How do I get to the football stadium?
A: Oh, that's easy. You . . .

2 *On the map, write the name of these places next to the* ***odd*** *numbers (1, 3, 5 etc.). Then answer your friend's questions.*

police station post office your house
swimming pool sports centre supermarket

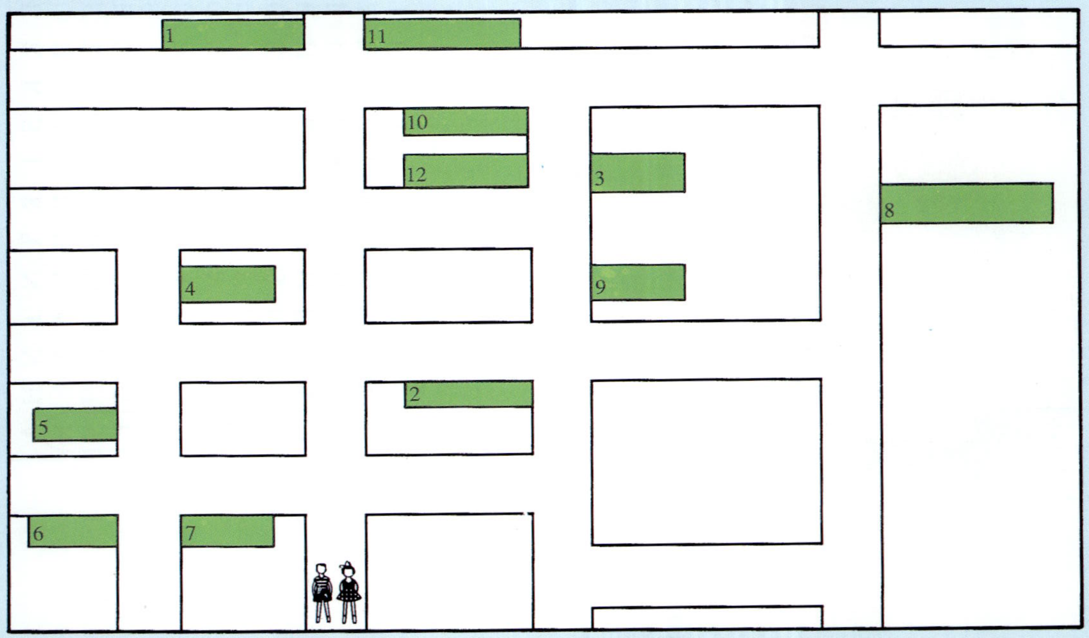

Unit 3

Chatterbox B

Chatterbox A see page *14*.

1 *Answer your friend's questions.*

2 *Ask your friend questions about Alan. Fill in the chart.*

▶ *eg* B: When does Alan go to the cinema?
A: He usually goes on Saturday but he sometimes goes on Sunday.

	always	usually	often	sometimes	never
go to the cinema		on Saturday		on Sunday	
go to the beach	in the summer		in the spring		
play tennis					
telephone friends					
clean his teeth					
ride a bike			at the weekend	on Tuesday afternoon	
go roller skating		on Sunday			on Monday
play volleyball					
do homework	before dinner				after dinner
read English books					
go to bed			before ten	after ten	

Unit 4

Chatterbox B

Chatterbox A see page *18*.

1 *Read.*

once a day   twice a week   three times a month
four times a year

2 *Answer your friend's questions.*

3 *Ask your friend questions about Mikis (M) and Jane (J). Fill in the chart.*

▶ *eg* B: How often does Mikis clean his teeth? (M2)
A: He cleans his teeth twice a day.
B: How often does Jane clean her teeth? (J3)
A: She cleans her teeth three times a day.

Action	Day	Week	Month	Year
clean teeth	J3 M2			
go to the dentist			J1	
play tennis		M1		
buy new records		J2		
play cards		M4		
go swimming		J1		
have a party				M1
go to a party			M2	
wash hair		J3		
ride a bicycle	M2			

Unit 6

Chatterbox B

Chatterbox A see page *24*.

1 *Answer your friend's questions about what Pedro and Françoise did.*

2 *Ask your friend questions. Fill in the chart.*

► *eg* B: What did Pedro do on Sunday morning?
A: He arrived in Rouen.

	Morning	Afternoon	Evening
Sunday 21	Pedro arrived in Rouen	They sat and talked	They
Monday 22	They visited the city	They watched TV	Pedro
Tuesday 23	They	They went shopping	They

	Morning	Afternoon	Evening
Wednesday 24	They went to Paris	They	They had dinner with Françoise's parents in Rouen
Thursday 25	Françoise and Pedro	Pedro arrived in Paris	Pedro

Chatterbox B

Chatterbox A see page *28*.

1 *Read the story and start to fill in the chart.*

2 *Answer your friend's questions.*

3 *Ask your friend questions and complete the chart.*

▶ *eg* B: What day are they going?
Where are they going in the afternoon?
What time are they going to get up?

Next week, on 26 July, the Bailey family – John and Anna Bailey and their two children – are going to Swansea. They are going to get up early and have a big breakfast of fried eggs and bacon. They are going to arrive in Swansea at nine o'clock. After looking at some paintings, they are going to do some shopping in the town centre and then they are all going to the sea. They are going to have a picnic lunch on the beach.

After lunch, Anna and her son are going to the centre of the town to visit Aunt Rose. She is very old and lives in a small house. Anna is going to take her some flowers and some chocolates.

All the family are going to meet in a café near the car at five o'clock. They are going to have some tea and cakes and then drive home to Cardiff for dinner.

Family's surname: ....
First names:
Father ....
Mother ....
Son ....
Daughter ....

Date of trip ....
Day of trip ....
Where/trip to? ....
How/travel? ....
How long/journey? ....

Time/get up? ....
What/breakfast? ....
Time/leave home? ....
Time/arrive Swansea? ....

Morning
Where/visit? ....
What/do then? ....
Time/go/beach? ....
What/do/beach? ....
Who/buy/sandwiches? ....
Where/lunch? ....

Afternoon
Father and daughter:
Where/go? ....
What/do? ....
Mother and son:
Where/go? ....
Who/visit? ....
What/take? ....
Family:
Where/meet? ....
Time/meet? ....
What/dinner? ....

Unit 8 — Chatterbox B

Chatterbox A see page *32*.

1 *Answer your friend's questions.*

2 *Ask your friend questions. Fill in the chart.*

▶ *eg* B: How far is the beach from the Teen Eye offices?
A: It's 120 kilometres.
B: How long does it take by car?
A: By car it takes 2 hours.

Place	Distance	Car	Bicycle	Foot
the beach	120 km	2 hours		19 hours
the cinema		10 minutes		25 minutes
the lake	16 km		50 minutes	
the bus stop		1 minute		3 minutes
the station	1.5 km		12 minutes	

Unit 9 — Chatterbox B

Chatterbox A see page *36*.

1 *Dictate the sentences in these dialogues to your friend. Say the words in groups.*

▶ *eg* That's a good idea!/
We can play football/
in the park.

2 *Ask your friend for the missing sentences in the dialogues. You may need to ask questions.*

▶ *eg* Can you repeat that, please?
How do you spell 'address', please?

Dialogue 1
A: ....
B: Yes, I'd love to./ Where do you live?
A: ....
B: Thank you./ Oh yes, I know the area.
A: ....
B: Is four o'clock all right?
A: ....
B: That's a good idea!/ We can play football/in the park.
A: ....
B: Great!/ Bye for now.

Dialogue 2
A: How far is your house/from the school?
B: ....
A: How long/does it take you/to get here/in the morning?
B: ....
A: How do you/come to school?
B: ....
A: No, I don't./ I come to school/by bus.
B: ....
A: Yes, I do./ I live near the park.
B: ....

Unit 11 — Chatterbox B

Chatterbox A see page *42*.

Susan wrote to Sally, one of Alan's cousins, to ask for some information about his family.

1 *Read Sally's answer and fill in more of the Bailey family tree on page 39.*

```
Dear Susan,
Thank you for your letter.  I think this is the information
you want.
    My name is Sally.  I live in Bristol with my father and
my brother, John.  My mother died in 1980.
    I am 13 years old and I was born in Swansea.  My brother
is 12 and he was born in the house we live in now.
    I have five cousins - Bill, Mary, Philip, Alan and
Sarah.  Bill and Alan are the same age as me.  Mary is my
favourite cousin.  She was born in Newcastle and her family
lives there still.  Her father, Michael, is my mother's
brother.  He was born in Bristol in 1946 and he married Aunt
Diane in 1971.
    Uncle John and his family live in Cardiff.  Uncle John's
wife, Teresa, is Italian. She was born in Olbia, in
Sardinia, in 1952.
I hope this information helps you.
Best wishes,
    Sally
```

2 *Answer your friend's questions.*

3 *Ask your friend questions and complete the family tree.*

► *eg* B: What is Alan's sister's name?
A: Her name is Sarah.
B: When was Michael's first son born?
A: He was born in 1978.
B: Where was Michael's wife born?
A: She was born in London.

Unit 12 — Chatterbox B

Chatterbox A see page *46*.

1 *Answer your friend's questions.*

2 *Find the secret message! Ask your friend questions and complete the sentences.*

► *eg* B: What do you know about Hollywood?
A: A lot of actors live in Hollywood.

A lot of actors l|i|ve in Hollywood.
Elephants are too big to |t|ravel by bus.
The English ___'_ __|_|__ ____ ____.
Teen Eye i|s| a TV programme.
There isn't much suns|h|ine in Finland.
Mosquitoes ____'_ ___ __|_|___ __ _____ _______.
Pedro is old enough |t|o travel alone.
The Portuguese ___'_|_|____ ____.
_____'_ _ ___ __ milk|_|_ _________.
The Irish dri|n|k a lot of milk.
Each day of the week has |g|ot a different name.
___ children __|_|__ __ _____.
Every country has got a di|f|ferent flag.
All Chinese eat |r|ice.
Amsterdam __ |_|_ ___ ___________.
Ice __ ___ |_|___ __ ___.
There aren't m|a|ny zoos in Italy.

Unit 13 *Chatterbox B*

Chatterbox A see page *50.*

1 *Read the story and ask your friend for the missing names.*

► *eg* B: Who went to the cinema with Beatrix and Karin?
A: Mikis did.

2 *Answer your friend's questions.*

Last Friday afternoon Mikis, Beatrix and Karin went to the cinema. Mikis and Beatrix met at the Teen Eye offices and .... waited at the cinema.
Mikis and Karin liked the film very much. After the film they all went to Hamburger Heaven. .... had a hamburger, Karin had a cheeseburger and .... had a fishburger. .... and .... drank water and Mikis had a cola.
In the evening they went to Jane's house and Mikis and Jane played cards. .... watched television and Karin wrote a letter to her mother. At about eight o'clock Jane took Beatrix home in her car and .... went home by bus. Karin telephoned for a taxi.

Unit 14 *Chatterbox B*

Chatterbox A see page *54.*

1 *Look at the note from Alan's mum about cleaning his untidy room. Answer your friend's questions.*

2 *Ask your friend questions and fill in the note.*

► *eg* B: What did he have to put on the bedside table?
A: He had to put the clock there.
B: Where did he have to put the clock?
A: He had to put it on the bedside table.

Alan
Before you go out you MUST put the

clock – bedside table
.... – shelf
encyclopedia – bookcase
.... – drawer
jeans – wardrobe
shoes – cupboard
school bag – ....
pen/pencils – desk
posters – ....
exercise books – school bag
.... – wardrobe
.... – drawer

Mum

Unit 16 Chatterbox B

Chatterbox A see page *60*.

1 *Ask your friend questions about the Suny television and fill in the chart.*

► *eg* B: How wide is the Suny TV?
A: It's ninety centimetres wide.

Television	wide	high	cost	age	screen size
Suny					
Ati					

2 *Look at the picture of the Ati television and fill in the chart. Then answer your friend's questions.*

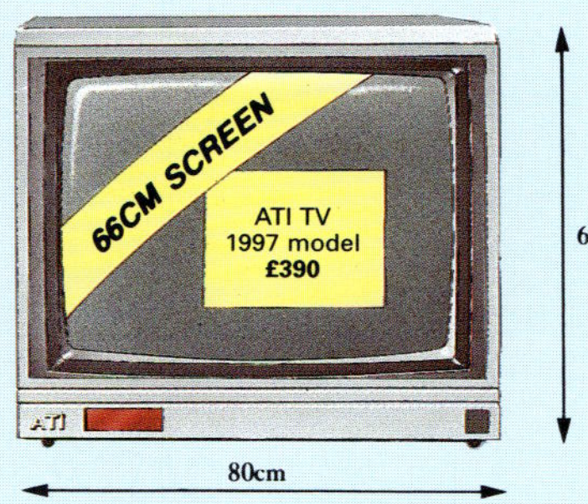

3 *Complete these sentences using is or isn't.*

a. The Suny television .... as new as the Ati.
b. The Ati television .... as high as the Suny.
c. The Suny television .... as cheap as the Ati.
d. The Ati television .... as wide as the Suny.
e. The Suny screen .... as big as the Ati.

4 *Read your sentences to your friend. Are your sentences the same?*

Unit 17 Chatterbox B

Chatterbox A see page *64*.

1 *Answer your friend's questions about the Asian elephant.*
How tall/How heavy/How wide/What colour

2 *Ask your friend questions about the African elephant. Fill in the chart.*

3 *Prepare and give a one-minute talk about the difference between an African and an Asian elephant.*

African elephant
Height: ....
Weight: ....
Colour: ....
....
....
Ears: .... wide
Origin: ....
....

Asian elephant
Height: 2.7 metres
Weight: 3,200–5,440 kg
Colour: light grey – some have pink or white spots on their skin
Origin: India, Borneo, mainland of Southeast Asia, Sri Lanka and Sumatra

Chatterbox B

Chatterbox A see page *68*.

1 *Answer your friend's questions.*

2 *Ask your friend questions and fill in the chart.*

► *eg* B: How many eggs does the average Briton eat each year?
A: The average Briton eats 236 eggs each year.

Nationalities			
		Singular	*Plural*
Britain	=	Briton	the British
France	=	Frenchman/woman	the French
Italy	=	Italian	the Italians
Russia	=	Russian	the Russians
Australia	=	Australian	the Australians
Japan	=	Japanese	the Japanese
Ireland	=	Irishman/woman	the Irish
America	=	American	the Americans

	Eggs	**Milk** *litres*	**Fish** *kilos*	**Beer** *pints*	**Fruit** *kilos*
Britain	236	111	5		53
France	277			71	
Italy		59	8.5		123
Russia	234			42	
Australia		148	8		93
Japan	262			69	
Ireland		156	12		53
America	266			171	

3 *Talk about the countries with your friend.*

► *eg* The French drink more milk than the Japanese but less than the British.
The Irish drink the most milk and the Japanese the least.

4 *Use information from the chart and compare three countries.*

Unit 19 — *Chatterbox B*

Chatterbox A see page *72.*

Next Saturday Derek will go to Copenhagen, in Denmark, to see the Teen Eye agent and Karin.

1 *Answer your friend's questions.*

2 *Ask your friend questions and fill in the chart.*

▶ *eg* B: What time will he leave home on Saturday?
A: He'll leave home at seven o'clock.
B: What will he do at two o'clock on Saturday?
A: He'll phone Fatma in London.

Saturday	
....	leave home
8.00	arrive at airport
9.30	....
11.00	plane lands at Copenhagen
12.00	....
12.30	arrive at hotel
2.00	....
2.30	meet Teen Eye agent
3.30	....
4.00	meet Karin
5.30	....

Sunday	
....	get up
....	meet Karin
9.00	drive to Open Air Museum
....	visit museum
12.30	return to Copenhagen
....	take photographs of city
5.00	say goodbye to Karin
....	get bus to airport
6.30	....
8.00	plane takes off
10.30	....
12.00	get home

Unit 21 — *Chatterbox B*

Chatterbox A see page *78.*

Last Friday was a terrible day for Pedro because everything broke!

1 *Ask your friend questions about the missing pictures. Write sentences.*

▶ *eg* B: What happened while Pedro was brushing his teeth?
A: While Pedro was brushing his teeth his toothbrush broke.
B: What was Pedro doing when his toothbrush broke?
A: When his toothbrush broke he was brushing his teeth.

These words will help you:

1. brush hair 2. shoelace 3. walk to door
4. handle 3. go down in lift 4. chain

2 *Answer your friend's questions.*

1. 
2. 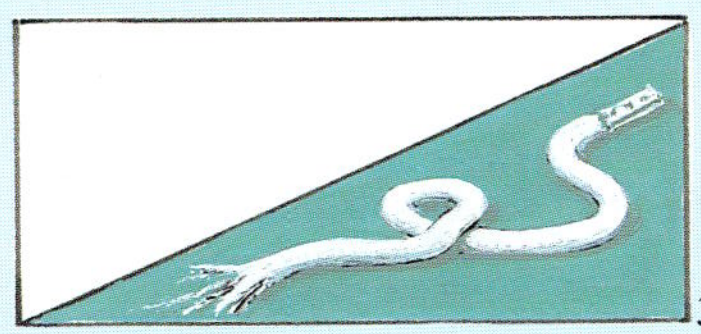
3. 
4. 
5. 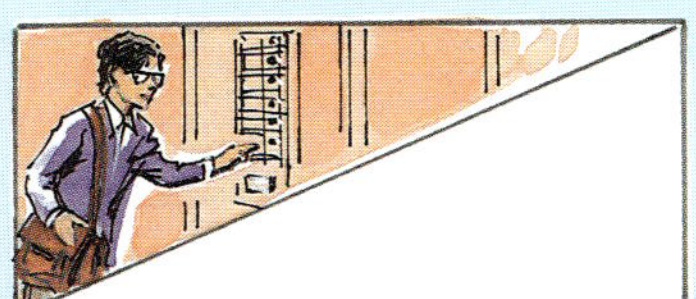
6. 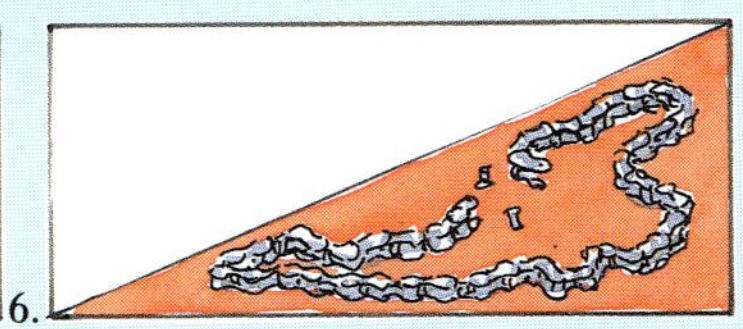

Unit 22 — Chatterbox B

Chatterbox A see page *82*.

1 *Listen to the dialogues in Unit 22a and Unit 22b again and tick (√) or cross (×) the information about Pedro.*

2 *Answer your friend's questions about Eric.*

3 *Ask your friend about Paul and fill in the chart.*

► *eg* A: Has Paul ever broken his leg?
B: Yes, he has./No, he hasn't.

4 *Write sentences about Pedro.*

► *eg* He's never broken his arm, but he's broken his leg.

	Pedro	Eric	Paul		Pedro	Eric	Paul
Broken: leg		√		**Illness:** scarlet fever		√	
finger		√		rubella		√	
arm		√		whooping cough		×	
ankle		×		mumps		√	
nose		√		chicken pox		×	
toe		×		measles		×	

Unit 23 — Chatterbox B

Chatterbox A see page *86*.

How long has everybody been at the Teen Eye office today?

1 *Read the text. Fill in as much of the chart as you can.*

2 *Ask your friend questions and fill in the rest of the chart.*

► *eg* B: Who arrived at half past eight?
A: Bill did.

Note: *Sometimes more than one person arrived at the same time.*

3 *Write two sentences each about Beatrix, Karin, Alan, Mikis, Fatma, Françoise, Pedro, Jane and Derek.*

► *eg* Bill has been at the office since half past eight.
Bill has been at the office for three and a half hours.

Bill, the doorman at the Teen Eye offices, was the first to arrive this morning. He arrived at half past eight. Jane arrived at the office half an hour after Derek. Karin, Mikis and Françoise all arrived together at eleven o'clock, half an hour before Beatrix. The time is now twelve o'clock.

Time	Name(s)
8.30	
9.00	
9.30	
10.00	
10.30	
11.00	
11.30	

Chatterbox B

Chatterbox A see page *90*.

1 *Answer your friend's questions about Alan.*

2 *Ask your friend questions about Alan and fill in the chart.*

▶ *eg* B: Has Alan been to the zoo recently?
A: Yes, he has. He's been there this month.
B: Has he eaten Spanish food recently?
A: No, he hasn't. He ate it over a year ago.

Activity	over two years ago	over a year ago	this month	this week
go/zoo			√	
eat/Spanish food		√		
play/basketball				
buy/new satchel				
go/seaside				√
visit/relations	√			
eat/Greek food				
play/handball			√	
visit/sick friend				
buy/new bicycle		√		
go/Brussels				
eat/French bread				√

Grammar summary

1 Verb **to be**: present tense

<table>
<tr><th colspan="3">Affirmative</th><th colspan="3">Negative</th><th colspan="3">Interrogative</th></tr>
<tr><td>I</td><td>am
’m</td><td rowspan="3">Portuguese.
thirteen years old.</td><td>I</td><td>am not
’m not</td><td rowspan="3">Danish.</td><td>Am</td><td>I</td><td rowspan="3">French?</td></tr>
<tr><td>You
We
They</td><td>are
’re</td><td>You
We
They</td><td>are not
’re not</td><td>Are</td><td>you
we
they</td></tr>
<tr><td>She
He
It</td><td>is
’s</td><td>She
He
It</td><td>is not
isn’t</td><td>Is</td><td>she
he
it</td></tr>
</table>

2 Verb **to be**: past tense

<table>
<tr><th colspan="3">Affirmative</th><th colspan="3">Negative</th><th colspan="3">Interrogative</th></tr>
<tr><td>I</td><td>was</td><td rowspan="3">at home.</td><td>I</td><td>was not
wasn’t</td><td rowspan="3">at home.</td><td>Was</td><td>I</td><td rowspan="3">at home?</td></tr>
<tr><td>You
We
They</td><td>were</td><td>You
We
They</td><td>were not
weren’t</td><td>Were</td><td>you
we
they</td></tr>
<tr><td>She
He
It</td><td>was</td><td>She
He
It</td><td>was not
wasn’t</td><td>Was</td><td>she
he
it</td></tr>
</table>

3 Verb **can**: present tense

<table>
<tr><th colspan="3">Affirmative</th><th colspan="3">Negative</th><th colspan="3">Interrogative</th></tr>
<tr><td>I
You
We
They
She
He
It</td><td>can</td><td>play billiards.</td><td>I
You
We
They
She
He
It</td><td>cannot
can’t</td><td>play chess.</td><td>Can</td><td>I
you
we
they
she
he
it</td><td>play chess?</td></tr>
</table>

4 Present simple tense

<table>
<tr><th colspan="4">Affirmative</th><th colspan="5">Negative</th><th colspan="5">Interrogative</th></tr>
<tr><td>I
You
We</td><td>come</td><td rowspan="2">from</td><td rowspan="2">France.
Spain.
Denmark.</td><td>I
You
We</td><td>do not
don’t</td><td rowspan="2">come</td><td rowspan="2">from</td><td rowspan="2">France.
Spain.
Denmark.</td><td>Do</td><td>I
you
we</td><td rowspan="2">come</td><td rowspan="2">from</td><td rowspan="2">Denmark?
France?
Spain?</td></tr>
<tr><td>She
He
It</td><td>comes</td><td>She
He
It</td><td>does not
doesn’t</td><td>Does</td><td>she
he
it</td></tr>
</table>

5 Present progressive/continuous tense (as future)

Affirmative			Negative			Interrogative		
I	am ’m		I	am not ’m not		Am	I	
You We They	are ’re	going to the cinema tonight.	You We They	are not aren’t	playing tennis this afternoon.	Are	you we they	coming to the party tomorrow?
She He It	is ’s		She He It	is not isn’t		Is	she he it	

6 Past simple tense: regular verbs

Affirmative			Negative				Interrogative			
I You We They She He	walked cycled	to school.	I You We They She He	did not didn’t	walk cycle	to school.	Did	I you we they she he	walk cycle	to school?

7 Past simple tense: irregular verbs

Affirmative			Negative				Interrogative			
I You We They She He It	went	to a party.	I You We They She He It	did not didn’t	go	to a party.	Did	I you we they she he it	go	to a party?

8 Future form: **going to**

Affirmative				Negative				Interrogative			
I	am ’m			I	am ’m			Am	I		
You We They	are ’re	going to	eat an apple. drink a cola.	You We They	are ’re	not going to	eat an apple. drink a cola.	Are	you we they	going to	eat an apple? drink a cola?
She He It	is ’s			She He It	is ’s			Is	she he it		

9 Modal verb: **must**

<table>
<tr><th colspan="3">Affirmative</th><th colspan="3">Negative</th><th colspan="3">Interrogative</th></tr>
<tr><td>I
You
We
They
She
He</td><td>must</td><td>stop.</td><td>I
You
We
They
She
He</td><td>must not

mustn't</td><td>stop.</td><td>Must</td><td>I
you
we
they
she
he</td><td>stop?</td></tr>
</table>

10 Imperatives

Turn	right.	Don't	turn	right.
Go	straight on.	Don't	go	straight on.
Take	the first on the right.	Don't	take	the first right.

11 Possessive nouns (genitive)

It is	my sister's	bicycle.
He is	that boy's	father.
They are	Alan's	books.

12 Present simple + gerund

<table>
<tr><th colspan="3">Affirmative</th><th>Negative</th><th>Interrogative</th></tr>
<tr><td>I
You
We
They</td><td>like</td><td>collecting stamps.

painting pictures.</td><td rowspan="2">(as present simple tense)</td><td rowspan="2">(as present simple tense)</td></tr>
<tr><td>He
She
It</td><td>likes</td><td>catching balls.</td></tr>
</table>

13 Adverbs of frequency

<table>
<tr><td>I
You
We
They</td><td rowspan="2">always
usually
often
sometimes
never</td><td>play</td><td rowspan="2">tennis at the weekend.</td></tr>
<tr><td>He
She
It</td><td>plays</td></tr>
</table>

Adverbs of ability

<table>
<tr><td>I
You
We
They</td><td rowspan="2">can play the guitar</td><td rowspan="2">very well.

badly.</td></tr>
<tr><td>He
She
It</td></tr>
</table>

14 WH questions

Where	do	you come from?
What	does	this mean?
Who	did	you stay with?
What time	did	they go?
When	did	he return?
How long	does	it take?
How	do	you spell it?
How much	does	it cost?
Why	did	she do it?
Whose dress	is	it?

15 Functions

Formal Invitation	Would you like to go to the cinema?	Yes, I'd love to. I'd love to but I can't.
Informal Invitation	Do you want to play tennis?	
Suggestions	Why don't we go to the cinema? What about going to the cinema?	

16 Verb **to be born**: past passive tense

<table>
<tr><td>Where</td><td>were</td><td>you
they</td><td rowspan="2">born?</td><td>I
You
We
They</td><td>were</td><td rowspan="2">born in France.</td></tr>
<tr><td>When</td><td>was</td><td>your father</td><td>He
She
It</td><td>was</td></tr>
</table>

17 too . . ./not . . . enough

<table>
<tr><td>I</td><td>am</td><td rowspan="3">not</td><td rowspan="3">small
big
hot
cold</td><td rowspan="3">enough.</td><td>I</td><td>am</td><td rowspan="3">too</td><td rowspan="3">small.
big.
hot.
cold.</td></tr>
<tr><td>You
We
They</td><td>are</td><td>You
We
They</td><td>are</td></tr>
<tr><td>He
She
It</td><td>is</td><td>He
She
It</td><td>is</td></tr>
</table>

18 Quantifiers: **much, many, a lot of**

<table>
<tr><td colspan="4">Affirmative</td><td colspan="4">Negative</td><td colspan="4">Interrogative</td></tr>
<tr><td rowspan="3">There</td><td>is</td><td rowspan="3">a lot of</td><td>cola.</td><td rowspan="3">There</td><td>isn't</td><td>much</td><td>cola.</td><td>Is</td><td rowspan="3">there</td><td>much</td><td>cola?</td></tr>
<tr><td rowspan="2">are</td><td rowspan="2">pens.</td><td rowspan="2">aren't</td><td rowspan="2">many</td><td rowspan="2">pens.</td><td rowspan="2">Are</td><td>many</td><td>pens?</td></tr>
<tr><td>a lot of</td><td>chalk?</td></tr>
</table>

19 Distributives: **each, all, every**

Each girl wears a badge. All the chocolate is soft. All the books are in English. Every class is full.

20 Past progressive/continuous tense

What	were	you they	doing at six o'clock?
	was	he she	

We They	were	eating an apple.
I He She It	was	

21 Subject question: **who**

Who	saw	you?	Alan did.
	told	her?	She did.

22 Past obligation: **had to**

Affirmative	Negative	Interrogative
I had to stop.	I didn't have to stop.	Did I have to stop?

23 Comparatives: **as . . . as**

The man	is	as	old	as	the woman.
The pears	are		expensive		the oranges.

24 Indefinite pronouns

Affirmative			Negative			Interrogative		
There is	somebody someone something nothing nobody no-one	near the tree.	There isn't	anybody anyone anything	near the tree.	Is there	anybody anyone anything	near the tree?

25 Comparative adjectives

The girl	is	older	than	the boy.
Football		more popular		cricket.
The film		more exciting		the book.
The women	are	taller		the men.

26 Irregular comparative adjectives

Peter	eats	more/fewer	chocolates	than	Alan.
	drinks	less	cola		
	has	better/worse	handwriting		

27 Superlative adjectives

It's	the	richest most expensive	country in the world.

28 Irregular superlatives adjectives

He	drinks eats	the	most least	milk. cheese.
	has		fewest	brothers.
			best worst	car. bicycle.

29 Future form: **will**

Affirmative				
I You He She It We You They	will 'll	travel be	to in	Paris next Friday.

Negative				
I You He She It We You They	will not won't	travel be	to in	Paris next Friday.

Interrogative				
Will	I you he she it we you they	travel be	to in	Paris next weekend?

30 Adjectives and verbs about weather

It will be	hot cold sunny windy cloudy foggy	tomorrow. next winter.
It will	snow rain	

31 Function

Asking about the weather
What will the weather be like? What's the weather going to be like? What's the weather like today? What was the weather like last week?

32 Infinitive of purpose: **to** + verb

how (verb)		where	why
I He	went drove	to the sea to England	to have a holiday. to learn English.

33 Interrupted past continuous/progressive tense

Past continuous + past simple + **when** or **while** Past continuous + past continuous + **when** or **while**
What was he doing **when** you arrived?
He was reading a book **when** I arrived. or **When** I arrived he was reading a book. or **While** he was reading a book I arrived.
What was he doing **while** you were watching television?
While I was watching television he was cleaning his shoes. or I was watching television **while** he was cleaning his shoes.

34 Present perfect tense

Affirmative				
I You We They	have	just already	seen	Peter.
			broken	a pencil.
			telephoned.	
He She It	has		had	measles.

Negative				
I You We They	have not haven't	seen	Peter	for six weeks.
		broken	a pencil	
		telephoned		recently.
He She It	has not hasn't	had	measles	since 1989.

Interrogative				
Have	I you we they	ever	broken	a pencil?
			seen	Peter?
			telephoned?	
Has	he she it		had	measles?

Irregular verbs

Infinitive	Past tense form	Past participle
become	became	become
begin	began	begun
bite	bit	bitten
break	broke	broken
bring	brought	brought
build	built	built
buy	bought	bought
catch	caught	caught
come	came	come
do	did	done
drink	drank	drunk
drive	drove	driven
eat	ate	eaten
fall	fell	fallen
feed	fed	fed
feel	felt	felt
find	found	found
fly	flew	flown
get	got	got
go	went	gone
have	had	had
hear	heard	heard
hit	hit	hit
hold	held	held
know	knew	known
leave	left	left
lose	lost	lost
make	made	made
meet	met	met
put	put	put
read	read	read
run	ran	run
say	said	said
see	saw	seen
send	sent	sent
sit	sat	sat
sleep	slept	slept
speak	spoke	spoken

Infinitive	Past tense form	Past participle
stand	stood	stood
swim	swam	swum
take	took	taken
tell	told	told
think	thought	thought
throw	threw	thrown
wake up	woke up	woken up
wear	wore	worn
win	won	won
write	wrote	written

Tapescripts

Unit 1a

Exercise 1

Fatma Good morning, everybody. My name is Fatma Barclay.
All Good morning.
Fatma Please call me Fatma. I'm the producer of the Teen Eye programmes. This is Derek – Derek Farley.
Derek Hello, everybody.
All Hello.
Fatma Derek is the programme director and that's Jane Adams. Jane is the programme co-ordinator.
Jane Hello, everybody. Nice to see you!
Fatma Right. Now, please come to the front in turn. I want to ask you some questions and fill in some forms. You come first. That's right – you. What's your name, please?

Exercise 2

Fatma What's your name, please?
Pedro My name's Pedro.
Fatma And what's your surname, Pedro?
Pedro Alves.
Fatma Can you spell that, please?
Pedro Yes, that's A-L-V-E-S.
Fatma A-L-V-E-S. Thank you. Where do you come from?
Pedro I come from Lisbon in Portugal.
Fatma Oh, you're Portuguese! And how old are you?
Pedro I'm thirteen.
Fatma What's your favourite hobby, Pedro?
Pedro I like music.
Fatma Do you like pop music?
Pedro Yes, I do. And I like playing the guitar.
Fatma Thank you, Pedro. Now, who's next?

Unit 1b

Exercise 1

Françoise Derek, where does Alfonso come from?
Derek He comes from Spain.
Françoise Does he live in Barcelona?
Derek No, he doesn't. He lives in Madrid, the capital city.
Françoise How old is he?
Derek He's fourteen, I think. Yes, fourteen.
Françoise And Karin? What nationality is she?
Derek She's Danish. She comes from Denmark.
Françoise Does she live in Copenhagen?
Derek Yes, she does.
Françoise And how old is she?
Derek She's twelve years old.
Françoise What's her favourite hobby?
Derek I don't know. You ask her!

Unit 2a

Exercise 3

Mikis What do you do on Wednesday afternoons, Alan?
Alan I play billiards.
Mikis Oh, I play billiards too. Where do you play?
Alan I play at St Mark's School.
Mikis Can I come with you next Wednesday?
Alan Yes, of course, Mikis. That's a great idea!

Unit 2b

Exercise 3

Beatrix Excuse me, Officer. How do I get to Rue du Marais?
Policeman Ah, Rue du Marais. That's easy. Go straight on and take the third turning on the left. Then turn first right. That's the Rue du Marais. What number do you want?
Beatrix Number 14. The Teen Eye offices.
Policeman Oh I know where they are. Number 14. Yes, it's the fourth building on the left.
Beatrix Thank you, officer.
Policeman My pleasure. Have a good day!

Unit 2c

Exercise 2

Pedro Jane, how do you organise the programmes?
Jane Well, every programme is a little different but generally it works like this. *First* we plan one year ahead. We choose subjects for each programme. The Teen Eye team, and that includes you of course, help us, here in Brussels, to choose the subjects for each programme.
Pedro What happens next?
Jane Well, *next* we collect all the film and photographs that we have in our library on the programme subject. We have a big film library here in the studio. *Then* we write the script for the programme *and*, at this point, we often realise that we need more film *so* we go to locations in Britain or abroad to get extra film and information for the programme. We meet members of the Teen Eye team and discuss the programme with them. Your ideas are very useful as, of course, you know more about the interests of young people in your countries than we do.
Pedro And when you have got all the film – then what happens?
Jane Well, *after that* we return to the studio and complete the script. *Then* with the script, the film and the photographs we produce the programme.
Pedro How long does that take?
Jane Oh, it takes about one week to complete. *And then*, when the programme is finished, we transmit it to the satellite. The satellite sends it to stations in countries all over the world. *Then* it is recorded and sent out to the local TV stations at a later date. Some countries put sub-titles in their own language on the programmes but the majority send it out in the original form.

Unit 3a

Exercise 2

Beatrix Oh, that's a lovely photo! Mother, father and two children.
Alan Two foals, you mean.
Beatrix Yes, I know.
Derek Do you ever go horse-riding, Beatrix?
Beatrix Yes, I go at the weekend. I go to the country with my sister Annie.
Derek Does she ever go horse-riding?
Beatrix No. She's only two years old.
Derek Do you ever go horse-riding, Alan?
Alan No, but I do athletics and I go swimming.
Derek Do you ever go swimming, Beatrix?
Beatrix No, but I go roller skating.
Derek What a lot of sports you both do!

Unit 3b

Exercise 1

Mikis What do you do in your spare time, Karin?
Karin I sometimes go swimming and I play tennis.
Mikis How often do you play tennis?
Karin Oh, I usually play twice a week in the summer.
Mikis Do you ever go roller skating?
Karin No, never. But I often go ice skating in the winter. It's very popular in Denmark. What about you?
Mikis I never go ice skating but I often go roller skating.
Karin And athletics? Do you do athletics at school?
Mikis Oh, yes. I do the long jump.
Karin And the high jump? Do you do the high jump?
Mikis The high jump? No, never. It's too difficult!

Unit 3c

Exercise 1

Beatrix I've got a beautiful horse. His name is Trigger. Trigger lives in stables in the country near our home. I usually go to see him on Sunday. I get up early and my father takes me to the stables. When I arrive I often brush Trigger for half an hour and, of course, I often go riding – when it's not raining.
We sometimes ride to a little village called Driemond. I never ride alone. I go with a riding school.
When we don't ride to Driemond we sometimes ride to the lake. We often stop for a picnic lunch near the lake, but Trigger usually eats all my food and I'm always hungry when we go home.

Unit 4a

Exercise 3

Alan Excuse me. I want to hire a bicycle.
Woman Certainly. Those ones over there are for hire.
Alan The green one's nice. How much is it?
Woman It's 600 francs a week.
Alan That's a bit expensive.
Woman This blue one is 480 francs, and 100 francs deposit.
Alan OK. That's fine. Those gloves are beautiful. How much are they?
Woman They're not expensive. They're 280 francs.
Alan Oh, yes. That's quite cheap. OK. The blue bicycle and the gloves.
Woman What nationality are you?
Alan I'm British.
Woman How often do you ride a bicycle in England?
Alan Not often. I ride about three times a year.
Woman Oh dear!

Unit 4b

Exercise 2

Woman You must remember that in Belgium we ride on the opposite side of the road.
Alan Yes, I know.
Woman And some of the road signs and rules are different. Look at that picture on the wall.
Alan Oh, yes.
Woman What does that sign mean?
Alan It means you must stop.
Woman Good. And that sign?
Alan You must turn left.
Woman OK. And that sign?
Alan Oh, I don't know. What does it mean?
Woman When you see this sign, it means you mustn't ride your bicycle there.
Alan Oh, I see.
Woman Now, look at number 6 in the picture. What's the rule?
Alan You mustn't carry big or heavy things on a bicycle.
Woman Very good. You know the rules. Here's the bicycle.

Unit 4d

Exercise 1

One
Beatrix That sign means there's a hospital near here. So we must be quiet!
Choose picture one now.

Two
Policeman You must turn left here and go to the corner. Then turn right and the cinema is on your left.
Choose picture two now.

Three
Karin Today is Wednesday. I must take my skates to school today because I go skating on Wednesday after school.
Choose picture three now.

Four
Alfonso I mustn't go to bed late today. I have an English examination in the morning.
Choose picture four now.

Five
Woman I must fill in this form with your name and address.
Choose picture five now.

Six
Françoise That sign means you mustn't leave your bicycle here.
Choose picture six now.

Seven
Pedro There's a tennis competition at the Youth Club next Saturday. I must buy a new racket.
Choose picture seven now.

Unit 5

Exercise 4

Part One

Linda Hello! I'm Linda Rose. The programme today is about pets. A lot of people have pets. From dogs to cats and birds many houses have an extra member of the family. Some people keep tortoises, hamsters and even snakes as pets. We sometimes read about pet lions, usually because they escape and walk around the streets of a town!
In the first part of the programme we are going to visit a pet shop. Andrew Duncan is thirteen. He lives in Aberdeen, a town in the north of Scotland. He has got a Saturday job. He works in a pet shop. Here, he is talking to our reporter, Mike Lessing.

Exercise 5

Part Two

Mike Andrew, you start work very early, don't you?
Andrew Yes, that's right. The shop opens at nine o'clock but I usually start work at about 7.30.
Mike Why do you start so early in the morning?
Andrew I must do a lot of things before the shop opens.
Mike Tell me about your day. What must you do?
Andrew Well, first I must open the shop door very carefully.
Mike Why?
Andrew Because animals sometimes escape during the night. They mustn't get out of the shop.
Mike Yes, of course. Then you go into the shop and your day starts.
Andrew Oh, yes. I close the door and then I must feed the animals. We usually give the cats and dogs biscuits mixed with tins of their special food, so the first thing I must do is open all the tins of food.
Mike OK. So the first thing you must do is to feed the cats and dogs. And then what do you do?
Andrew When the cats and dogs are eating, I clean the bird cages and then give them seed and water.
Mike So, first you feed the cats and dogs and then you clean the cages and feed the birds. Is that right?
Andrew Yes, that's right. Then I take the dogs out for a quick walk in the

garden behind the shop. Then I take them back to the shop and brush them. I must make them look beautiful for the customers in the shop.

Mike Obviously. Then what do you do?

Andrew I feed the other animals. I give salad to the rabbits, vegetables to the hamsters and fish food to the fish. When all the animals are eating and happy, I start cleaning the shop. I wash the floor and clean all the cages.

Mike Do you like your job?

Andrew It's fantastic! I know all the animals and they know me. They're my friends!

Unit 6a

Exercise 1

Sarah What are you doing tonight?

Alan I'm watching a programme on television.

Sarah What's it about?

Alan It's about the Dutch royal family.

Sarah What! Why are you interested in them?

Alan I'm giving a talk to my class next Wednesday.

Sarah Oh dear! How long are you speaking for?

Alan I'm speaking for about ten minutes.

Sarah How awful! What's your talk about?

Alan About foreign royal families.

Sarah Well, good luck! I hate giving talks in the classroom.

Unit 6b

Exercise 2

Mikis Can you swim, Karin?

Karin Yes, I can.

Mikis How well can you swim?

Karin I can swim very well. I go to the swimming pool three times a week.

Mikis Can you roller skate?

Karin No, I can't. Not at all. Can you skate?

Mikis Yes, I can, but I skate badly. I try and try, but I can't stand up.

Karin Can you play tennis?

Mikis Yes, I can. Can you?

Karin Yes, I can.

Mikis Oh, good. Let's have a game this afternoon!

Karin That's a good idea!

Unit 6c

Exercise 2

Part One

Beatrix Where are you going next Christmas?

Alan I'm going to Sardinia.

Beatrix Sardinia? Who are you staying with?

Alan I'm staying with my cousin Antonio.

Beatrix Your cousin? But you're Welsh, aren't you?

Alan Yes, but my mother's Italian, from Sardinia.

Beatrix How interesting! How long are you staying there?

Alan For ten days.

Exercise 4

Part Two

Beatrix Ten days in Sardinia! Fantastic! How are you getting there?

Alan Oh, it's very complicated.

Beatrix Why?

Alan Well, first we're driving from Cardiff to London. Then we're flying to Milan, in the north of Italy. From Milan we're going by bus from the airport to the station and then we're travelling by train from Milan to Genoa, a city on the coast.

Beatrix Wow! Car, plane, bus, train. Then what?

Alan Well from Genoa we're taking the ferry to Olbia in Sardinia.

Beatrix Can't you fly direct to Sardinia?

Alan Oh, yes. But there were no tickets left, and this way is much more exciting!

Unit 7a

Exercise 2

Jane You look tired, Derek. Where did you go last weekend?

Derek I went to the country.

Jane How nice. Where did you stay?

Derek I stayed with my aunt on her farm.

Jane Did you have a good time?

Derek Yes, I did. But I woke up very early every morning.

Jane Why? What happened?

Derek There was a cock on the farm.

Jane Oh, dear!

Derek It crowed at dawn every morning and, of course, I woke up.

Jane How awful!

Derek Yes, I got up at five o'clock every morning, and I was on holiday!

Unit 7b

Exercise 5

Boy a. Our teacher comes from England, doesn't he?
Our teacher comes from England, doesn't she?

Girl b. You're French, aren't you?

Boy c. You study English, don't you?

Girl d. Your friend's a very tall boy, isn't he?

Boy e. Our teacher wakes up early, doesn't he?
Our teacher wakes up early, doesn't she?

Girl f. You were in Spain last year, weren't you?

Boy g. He was good at English last term, wasn't he?

Girl h. They can swim well, can't they?

Unit 7c

Exercise 5

Alan Can I have a birthday party next week, Mum?

Mother Yes, that's a good idea. On Saturday afternoon.

Sarah Can I invite my friends?

Alan No, Sarah, you can't. It's my birthday party.

Mother Oh, Alan. Let your sister invite one friend.

Alan OK. One friend!

Sarah One friend! Who am I going to invite? I want to invite Mary and Carol and John . . .

Alan Quiet, Sarah. Mum said one friend.

Sarah Oh all right. I'm going to invite Carol.

Alan Good. Now, let me think.

Mother What are you going to eat?

Alan Oh, sandwiches and some crisps.

Mother What are you going to drink, Alan?

Alan Cola is fine.

Mother What are you going to do at the party?

Alan Oh, lots of things. We're going to dance, talk, eat and drink.

Mother And who are you going to invite?

Alan Friends from school and from Teen Eye. About thirty people. Is that all right?

Mother Yes, OK. But no more.

Unit 8a

Exercise 3

Jane Why don't we go to France next week?

Fatma That's a good idea!

Jane We can visit Françoise in Rouen.

Fatma Yes, I want some film of a French school.

Jane What about going to Paris afterwards?

Fatma I'd love to, but I can't. I must come back here for a meeting.

Jane What a pity!

Unit 8b

Exercise 1

Jane How far is Rouen from here?

Fatma Oh about a hundred and sixty kilometres.

Jane How long does it take to get there?

Fatma It depends on how you travel.

Jane Oh, yes. How long does it take by car?

Fatma By car? Why don't we go by train?

Jane Because there are no trains to Rouen this morning.

Fatma Oh I see. Well, by car it takes about two hours.

'ane That's OK. Let's hire a car then.

Unit 8c

Exercise 1

Derek What sports do young people play in European countries?
Jane Well, basketball is popular in Germany, but is it popular in Italy?
Derek I don't know. Maybe. What about ice skating? It's probably popular in cold countries like Sweden and Denmark, but do you think they ice skate in hot countries?
Jane It's possible. What about writing a questionnaire on sports?
Derek That's a good idea. We can send it to schools all over the world.
Jane Great! Then the information about the sports young people like and play comes directly from them.
Derek Yes. Can you prepare the questionnaire this afternoon?
Jane Yes. Certainly.
Derek I'm going to my office to write a letter to send to teachers with the questionnaire.

Unit 9a

Exercise 4

Beatrix Jane! Welcome to Amsterdam.
Jane It's lovely to see you.
Beatrix Come in. Did you have a good journey?
Jane Yes, it was fine. The trip from the airport was beautiful.
Beatrix What do you want to do this morning? Would you like to go to the Vincent van Gogh Museum?
Jane I'd love to. How far is it?
Beatrix It's not far from here. About ten minutes by train. Would you like to visit the flower market too?
Jane I don't think there's enough time this morning. The Vincent van Gogh Museum is very big.
Beatrix OK. We can go this afternoon.

Unit 9b

Exercise 2

Alan Hey, Pedro, let's play tennis this afternoon.
Pedro That's a great idea! Françoise, do you want to play tennis after lunch?
Françoise Yes, I'd love to!
Alan That's you, me and Françoise. Why don't you ask Alfonso too?
Pedro Alfonso!
Alfonso Yes? What is it?
Pedro Do you want to play tennis this afternoon?
Alfonso I'd love to but I can't. I must study. Ask Derek.
Alan That's a good idea. Ask him, Pedro.
Pedro No, you ask him.
Alan Don't be silly! Derek?
Derek Yes, Alan?
Alan Would you like to play tennis this afternoon?
Derek Yes, I'd love to. What time are you going to play?
Alan About half past three.
Derek That's fine. Let's meet outside the studios and go to the park.

Unit 9c

Exercise 3

Beatrix Mum!
Mum Yes?
Beatrix I've got lots of replies to my party invitations. Let's see. Anne can come and so can Pieter, but Margrit can't come. Oh! Here's a letter from Derek!
Mum Oh yes? What does it say? Read it to me.
Beatrix Um . . . Dear Beatrix. Thank you for your invitation. I am not working that weekend and so I would love to come to your party. I am sure it is going to be a very good party. I am looking forward to it and to meeting your family. With best wishes, Derek.
Mum Well, that's a nice letter, isn't it?
Beatrix Yes, but what a pity Jane can't come too.

Unit 9d

Exercise 1

My birthday is on April the 20th. When I was nearly thirteen years old and living in Green Lane, Oxford, I decided to have a birthday party. As April the 20th that year was on a Friday, I planned the party for the day after my birthday as we don't go to school on Saturdays in England.
I went to the newsagent's and bought twenty party invitations. At home, I wrote the addresses of twenty of my friends on the envelopes and then I filled in the invitation cards with my address and the date and time of the party and put them inside. Then I went to the post office and bought twenty stamps and took them home. I put the stamps on the envelopes and put all the invitations into a plastic bag to take to the post-box.
A week before the party my mother made me a beautiful new dress and I bought a new pair of shoes.
On the morning of the party I prepared the sitting room and later my mother made a lot of sandwiches. After that I went to the supermarket and bought some cola and orange juice.
At five o'clock, when the party started, none of my friends were there. I waited and waited and waited. 6.15 – 6.30 – seven o'clock. My friends didn't come. I decided to telephone my friend, Michael Green. Michael answered the phone. 'Party? What party?', he asked. I telephoned another friend, Carol. 'Party? What party?', she asked. Then I had an idea. I went into my bedroom and looked under my desk. There in the corner was the plastic bag with the invitations to my party! What a disaster!!

Unit 10

Exercise 6

Karin What are we going to do this weekend?
Mikis Why don't we go and visit somewhere new?
Karin That's a good idea. Let's go to Cambridge. We can stay the night in a youth hostel.
Mikis No, I went to Cambridge last year with my parents. I don't want to go there again.
Karin What about Scotland? There are some very fast trains from Euston to Inverness.
Mikis Great! We can travel overnight on Friday and stay Saturday and Sunday and come back on Monday.
Karin OK. Let's go to the Highlands. The Teen Eye team is preparing a programme on Scotland and I saw some brochures on Derek's desk.
Mikis What's so special about the Highlands?
Karin Oh, the photographs were wonderful. Beautiful mountains and green valleys.
Mikis It sounds a bit boring to me. What is there to do there?
Karin There's a new tourist park called Highland Mysteryworld near Fort William. There's lots to see and do there.
Mikis That sounds like fun.
Karin That's settled then. I'm going to phone the station and find out the times of the trains.
Mikis And I'm going to buy some maps of Scotland.
Karin So, a weekend in the Highlands. You never know, you might have some Scottish ancestors and be allowed to wear a kilt!
Mikis What, me in a skirt! You must be joking! Anyway, I don't think the ancient Greeks got as far as Scotland.

Unit 11a

Exercise 3

Susan How many children did your grandfather have, Alan?
Alan My father's father had three children: my father John, Uncle Michael and Aunt Mary.
Susan And when was your father born?
Alan He was born in 1950.

Susan Where was he born?
Alan He was born in Calcutta in India.
Susan How interesting! How many brothers and sisters have you got?
Alan I've got one sister, Sarah. She's ten.
Susan And your Aunt Mary, when was she born?
Alan She was born about 1945 and she died in 1980.
Susan Oh, I'm sorry.
Alan Aunt Mary and Uncle Freddie had two children.
Susan What are their names?
Alan John and Sally. They're my cousins.

Unit 11d

Exercise 2

Part One

At the end of a meal or a party in Russia everybody drinks a small glass of vodka. They say 'Thank you for the meal', 'Congratulations' or 'Good luck'. This is called a 'toast'. After a toast everybody throws their glass into the fireplace. The glasses break of course. This brings good luck.

Exercise 3

Part Two

A few years ago in Leningrad, Ludmila Romanov married Viktor Sidak. Viktor was the son of the director of Leningrad Museum.

Grigory Romanov, Ludmila's father, was mayor of Leningrad. He wanted a very special wedding party for his daughter. He visited Viktor's father at the museum. 'You have a beautiful tea-set in the museum. Can I use it at our childrens' party?' he asked.

'Of course, you can. I want our children to have a fantastic party. But remember, this is a very special tea-set. It was Catherine the Great's tea-set and it's very valuable.'

Mr Sidak put the cups, saucers and teapot into a big box and took it to Mr Romanov's house on the day of the party. 'Be very, very careful,' he said. 'I must return the tea-set to the museum tonight.'

All the party guests arrived and had a good time. They drank tea from Catherine the Great's teacups and ate cake on her plates. The party was nearly over. Grigory Romanov went into the kitchen to get the vodka glasses for the toast to Ludmila and Viktor. Suddenly one of the guests stood up and dropped his teacup on the floor. All the other guests thought it was the toast so they all threw their teacups into the fireplace! 'Good luck!' they all shouted.

Now in Leningrad Museum you can see Catherine the Great's saucers and plates but you can't see her teacups!

Unit 12a

Exercise 1

Alfonso Do you like my new bicycle, Pedro?
Pedro Yes. It's fantastic. But why is it so dirty?
Alfonso Oh, I can't put it in my garage.
Pedro Why not?
Alfonso There's not enough space for Dad's car *and* my bike.
Pedro Oh, so your garage is too small.
Alfonso No, it isn't. My Dad's car is too big!

Unit 12c

Exercise 3

Derek Is everything ready for the meeting this afternoon?
Jane Yes, I think so. Look in the cupboard over there. Is there any paper?
Derek Yes there is. There's a lot of ruled paper.
Jane Good. Is there much plain white paper?
Derek No, there isn't much. There's only half a packet.
Jane Mmmm. What about pens? Are there a lot of pens?
Derek Let me see. There aren't many blue pens, but there are a lot of black ones.
Jane Are there many red pens?
Derek No, there aren't any.
Jane Oh dear! Let's start again. I must list the things we haven't got enough of.

Unit 12d

Exercise 3

Alan Are you going to the fancy dress party on Friday?
Jane Of course I am.
Alan What are you going as?
Jane I'm dressing up as Snow White.
Alan Snow White! Beatrix is going as Snow White.
Jane Oh dear! I know, I'm going as a cowgirl.
Alan That's a good idea.
Jane What are *you* dressing up as?
Alan I'm going as a witch.
Jane Oh? What are you wearing?
Alan I'm wearing a very old black dress and a hat.
Jane What is Mikis dressing up as?
Alan Dracula, I think.
Jane Great. It's going to be a great party.

Unit 13a

Exercise 3

Susan Where were you at six o'clock yesterday?
Alan I was at Dan's house.
Susan What were you doing?
Alan I was helping Dan with his homework.
Susan What time did you arrive there?
Alan At about half past five.
Susan And what time did you leave?
Alan Leave? Oh about seven o'clock. Why?
Susan I telephoned you at quarter past six. I was doing my homework and I wanted some help.

Unit 13b

Exercise 1

Sarah I know you were at the bus stop in Hall Road yesterday evening.
Alan Who saw me?
Sarah My friend Ellen did.
Alan Oh, yes. At what time?
Sarah At about five o'clock.
Alan Hmm. Yes, that's right.
Sarah Well, what were you doing there?
Alan It's none of your business.
Sarah Were you going home?
Alan No, I wasn't.
Sarah Well, what were you doing there?
Alan Oh, sisters! I was waiting for Susan, my friend from school.
Sarah You were waiting for Susan at a bus stop!
Alan Yes, nosey! The bus stop is in front of her house!

Unit 13c

Exercise 2

Headmaster Oh, good morning, David. Where were you at ten o'clock this morning?
David I was in the library, sir.
Headmaster Why weren't you in class?
David I was getting a book for the teacher.
Headmaster What time were you in the library?
David At exactly ten o'clock, sir.
Headmaster How do you know it was exactly ten o'clock?
David When I heard the crash and the glass breaking, I looked at the clock in the library, the clock above the door, and the time was exactly ten.
Headmaster Oh, I see. And the time on the clock was ten? Thank you, David. You can go back to class now.
David Thank you, sir.
(*the door opens and closes*)
Headmaster Come in, Alan. Sit down over there. Now, why weren't you in your classroom at ten o'clock this morning?
Alan I was in the First Aid room, sir.
Headmaster The First Aid room! What were you doing there?

Alan I was waiting for the nurse. I cut my hand.
Headmaster Was the nurse with you at ten?
Alan No, sir. The First Aid room was empty. I was waiting for the nurse to arrive.
Headmaster And how do you know the time was exactly ten o'clock?
Alan I heard the bell in the school clock at ten. It's very loud and it's next to the First Aid room.
Headmaster Oh, I see. OK Alan, you can go back to class now.
Alan Thank you, sir.

Unit 14a

Exercise 3

Alan Why didn't you come to the handball match last Thursday?
Jerry I've got a lot of problems with maths and history at school.
Alan Did you have to do extra homework?
Jerry Yes, I did. I had to do twenty extra maths exercises, but I didn't have to do any extra history.
Alan Oh, I see. Well, it doesn't matter because there's another practice this afternoon.
Jerry But I can't come.
Alan Oh no, not extra homework again!
Jerry Yes, I have to do extra history homework today!

Unit 14b

Exercise 2

Beatrix How was your examination last week, Mikis?
Mikis Oh, that. It was very difficult.
Beatrix How many questions did you have to answer?
Mikis I had to answer six. Five grammar questions and one composition.
Beatrix Did you write a letter or a story?
Mikis I chose the story but it was very difficult.
Beatrix Why didn't you choose the letter?
Mikis Because I didn't understand the question!

Unit 14c

Exercise 3

Fatma You do a lot of athletics, don't you, Mikis?
Mikis Yes, that's right. I do both track and field events.
Fatma Which events do you like?
Mikis Well, in the field events I like the long jump and throwing the javelin and in the track events I like short distances, especially the 100 metres.
Fatma Do you practise a lot?
Mikis Yes, every afternoon in the summer. Last month I went to an Athletics Camp.
Fatma Athletics Camp? What's that?
Mikis Well, two or three sports clubs get together and we all go to camp.
Fatma What did you do there?
Mikis Well, our day started very early.
Fatma Oh, what time did you get up?
Mikis We had to get up at four o'clock every morning.
Fatma Wow! That's early!
Mikis Yes, very. Then we had to stand for a long time and the trainer, Mr Barnes, divided us into two groups. The track group and the field group.
Fatma I see. And then what did you do?
Mikis Well, the field group had to climb a mountain.
Fatma And the track group?
Mikis They had to run three kilometres.
Fatma That's not very far for athletes!
Mikis I know. But this is all before breakfast! When we returned to the camp, we had to shower and clean the tents before we had breakfast.
Fatma And after breakfast? What did you do then?
Mikis We practised sports all day.
Fatma It sounds like fun. Did you enjoy it?
Mikis Yes, I did.
Fatma What was your favourite time during the day?
Mikis Oh, definitely the evenings. We didn't have to go to bed early!
Fatma What did you do?
Mikis Oh, we sat around the camp-fire and sang songs until we were tired. It was fantastic.

Unit 15

Exercise 6

Bill Good morning Miss Barclay. How are you?
Fatma I'm fine, thanks, Bill.
Bill I saw you at the hospital last Friday.
Fatma Did you?
Bill Yes, I was sitting on the bus at about eleven o'clock and I saw you in the street. You were going into the hospital.
Fatma Oh, yes. That's right.
Bill Were you visiting a friend?
Fatma No, I wasn't. I had to go and see a doctor.
Bill Oh, you're all right, aren't you?
Fatma Yes, I'm fine now but I was ill last week.
Bill Why? What happened?
Fatma I went to a conference in Italy recently and a snake bit me.
Bill Oh, dear. Was it poisonous?
Fatma Yes, it was, but I had a special injection in Italy and then another last Friday at the hospital here. And now I feel perfect.
Bill Oh, I am glad. Have a nice day!
Fatma And you, Bill. And you!

Unit 16a

Exercise 2

Derek This is a very thick fog. I can't see anything.
Fatma Be careful! There's something on the left.
Derek Yes, I can see it. It's a man on a bicycle.
Fatma Whew! That was close. Look out on the right! There's something over there!
Derek I can't see anybody. It's too foggy.
Fatma It's not a person. It's a round object. Look! There!
Derek Fatma, I can't see anything at all.
Fatma It's near the corner.
Derek I can't see anything. There's nothing there.
(*There is a loud crash.*)
Derek Oh, dear! There was something there!
Fatma Yes, you killed a dustbin!

Unit 16b

Exercise 1

Beatrix And this is my bedroom.
Françoise Oh, Beatrix. It's beautiful!
Beatrix It isn't as big as your bedroom.
Françoise My bedroom isn't as comfortable as yours. You've got a sofa and a record player!
Beatrix Do you want to listen to some music?
Françoise Yes, that's a good idea.
Beatrix My records aren't as new as yours. I spend all my pocket money on horse-riding lessons.
Françoise You've got Michael Jackson's first record. Put that on.

Unit 16c

Exercise 2

Derek What about a novel for Mikis?
Jane That's a good idea.
Derek That Agatha Christie one looks exciting.
Jane It's not as exciting as that James Bond book. Let's buy that for Mikis.
Derek That's fine. Now, what about Beatrix?
Jane She wants a new bag. They're over there.
Derek This green one isn't as big as that red one but it isn't as expensive.
Jane Yes, the red one's very expensive. Let's get the green one.
Derek Now, who's next? Oh yes, Karin.
Jane I know she wants a dictionary.
Derek OK. Let's go back to the book department.
Jane This dictionary looks very good.
Derek Yes, it is but it's very heavy.
Jane True. What about this one? It's as

good as the other one but it isn't as heavy.

Derek That's settled then. Now, what about a present for Alfonso?

Jane He likes football. He wants a Manchester United scarf.

Derek Here they are. What about this one?

Jane It's nice but it's very long.

Derek And this one? It isn't as long but it's as warm as the other one because it's made of wool.

Jane That's great. Now, who's next . . .?

Unit 17a

Exercise 3

Pedro Let's see. Look at these maps, Fatma. Britain is a lot smaller than Australia, isn't it?

Fatma Yes, it is. But Britain has a bigger population than Australia.

Pedro Do people live longer in Britain or in Australia?

Fatma It's the same, isn't it?

Pedro Ah! – no, it isn't. Here it says that people live one year longer in Australia.

Fatma Maybe that's because the weather is better in Australia.

Pedro That's true. It's warmer in Australia than in Britain.

Fatma What about the cost of living, Pedro? Are things more expensive in Australia or in Britain?

Pedro Well, coffee is cheaper but a record is more expensive.

Fatma That's not very good.

Pedro Why?

Fatma I don't drink coffee but I buy a lot of records.

Unit 17d

Exercise 2

Linda Hello! I'm Linda Rose. Today we're at Taronga Zoo in Sydney, Australia. The Australians built the zoo in 1881 and moved it to here in 1916.
The zoo gets its animals in many different ways. Sometimes people find injured animals and bring them here. Sometimes they exchange animals with other zoos in the world. But most of the animals are born here.
Today we're going to look at birds and animals that we can find only in Australia.

Linda The first ones – here – are birds. They are kookaburras, but they are also called laughing jackasses because they sound like a person laughing. They are 47 cm long and their bills are about 10 cm in length. They are small and have white, brown, black and blue feathers. They live in families in forests and the parents live together in pairs.

Linda Let's move on . . . Now, these birds are emus. They're about 1.5 metres tall and weigh about 55 kg. They are larger than the kookaburra. Only the ostrich is larger than the emu in the bird world. The emu cannot fly, but it can run as fast as a kangaroo – 50 kilometres an hour! – and it can swim very well. The male bird does all the baby-sitting and feeding of the young for 18 months after the chicks are born.

Linda Now this one's interesting! This very strange animal is the duck-billed platypus. It has a bill like a duck. It's about 61 cm long and it weighs about 1.8 kg. The platypus duck (as it's sometimes called) swims using webbed feet. There is some poison in its feet. The poison can kill small animals.

Linda And, finally, here is the wombat. It is a large animal and it digs holes in the ground. Wombats are between 70 and 120 cm long and weigh up to 27 kg. They have short legs and no tail. They dig for food at night and sleep during the day.
Many farmers don't like wombats because the holes they make are bad for the farmers' animals and crops.

Unit 18a

Exercise 2

Pedro Hi, Jane! What are you doing?

Jane I'm working on the programme for next Easter.

Pedro What's it about?

Jane It's the programme called 'The Most'. Do you remember?

Pedro Oh, yes. That was my idea! The biggest and smallest things in the world.

Jane That's right. Well, we changed it a little but the idea was yours.

Pedro What biggest and smallest things are in the programme?

Jane We've got mountains, volcanoes and countries. But we've also got the richest and poorest country, the longest river and many other things.

Pedro The richest country? Which is the richest country in the world?

Jane The richest country in the world is Bermuda.

Pedro And the poorest?

Jane The poorest is . . . Here – read the script and learn some geography!

Unit 18c

Exercise 2

Presenter Gatwick Airport was originally a racecourse. It became an airport in 1930 and in 1958 it became London's second airport. Now Gatwick is one of the biggest airports in the world.
The air-traffic control tower at Gatwick Airport is the tallest in Europe. At the Information Desk, American travellers ask the most questions and Japanese travellers the fewest. The most popular questions are 'Where are the toilets?' and 'Where are the trains?'. The most frequent answers are 'Follow the signs!' and 'Behind you!'
Gatwick is a 'silent' airport. There are no announcements about the take-off and landing times of aeroplanes. Gatwick is more dangerous than many other airports because there is only one runway, but in an emergency fire engines can get to any part of the airport in less than three minutes.

Unit 19a

Exercise 2

Alan Derek, would you like to come to my house for dinner next Saturday?

Derek I'd love to but I won't be in England next weekend.

Alan Oh? Where will you be?

Derek I'll be in Denmark.

Alan That's nice. Will you be in England the Saturday after?

Derek Yes, I will. I'll return to London on Thursday.

Alan Would you like to come to dinner next Saturday week?

Derek Yes, that will be great. Thank your parents for me.

Unit 19c

Exercise 4

Forecaster Good afternoon. Here is the weather forecast for Europe tomorrow. It will snow in the north of Scotland and it will be foggy, especially in the early hours of the morning. Moving south to London, it will be very cold, temperatures about −7° Centigrade, but the sun will come out later in the day. It will be a cold bright day.

Across to Copenhagen and the weather will be very cold with some snow. Temperatures about the same as in London.

Moving south now, to mainland Europe. The weather will be quite good tomorrow. Amsterdam will have some rain in the morning and then the sun will appear. Berlin will be a little cloudy, and so will Warsaw, but it will be sunny after lunch.

In Brussels it will be sunny all day, but in Prague it will be windy and it will probably rain in the afternoon. It will be a beautiful day in Paris with sun all day, but south near Bordeaux it will be windy and it will rain.

The weather in south Europe will be very different tomorrow. In Madrid it will rain all day but in Barcelona it will be sunny. Across in Italy, Rome will be cloudy and cold. The weather in Milan, in the north, will be very similar with temperatures of −5. It will be cloudy all day but there will be no fog.

Going north to Switzerland, Zurich will have a windy day and it will snow in Munich, in Germany. Vienna, in the east, will have rain all day.

Unit 20

Exercise 2

Jane Let's make some notes about the history of food and drink.

Derek Here's the reference book but where do you want to start?

Jane Hmm. I know, what did you have for lunch today?

Derek I had a yoghurt. Why?

Jane Well, let's start there.

Derek OK. Let me see. Yoghurt. Ah, here it is. Yoghurt, 4500 BC. Asia.

Jane You mean people in Asia ate yoghurt six thousand five hundred years ago? I never knew that. It's incredible! So, let's start with that. What else have you got?

Derek Well, in 2750 BC the Chinese emperor, Chen-Nong, invented tea.

Jane So, yoghurt and tea. That's a good start.

Derek What about including wine? It says here that people started drinking wine in Crete and China about 2000 BC.

Jane Fine. Let's move on in time a little.

Derek How about this? In the year 850 BC in Ethiopia they started growing coffee beans and making coffee.

Jane So, we've got yoghurt, tea, wine and coffee. What about food?

Derek Let me see. Food, food. Oh, what about things for cooking? This is important. In 1860 a French scientist called Denis Papin invented the first pressure cooker.

Jane Yes, that's important but let's keep to food and drink, otherwise the programme is going to become too technical. Who's that picture of?

Derek It's a picture of John Montague, the Earl of Sandwich in England. Guess what he invented.

Jane That's easy, the first sandwich. What was the date?

Derek 1762. Here's another date for you. In 1860 Ferdinand Carré, a French engineer, built the first fridge.

Jane You do like machines, don't you! What about things we eat and drink today?

Derek Well, in 1886 John Pemberton invented Coca Cola, then two years later Keith Kellogg started selling cornflakes.

Jane That's more interesting. Are there any other names like Kellog's?

Derek Here's one. In 1915 Clarence Birdseye invented a new method for freezing food.

Jane Great! Look there. What's that about Tetra Pak?

Derek What's Tetra Pak?

Jane It's a special container for liquids like milk and fruit juice.

Derek Oh, yes. I know. Let's see. Tetra Pak made the first containers in 1961. I always find them so difficult to open. But listen to this. In 1994 they sold seventy-three billion of them in a hundred and twenty-four countries!

Jane So they got that right even if you can't open them!

Derek Oh, all right. Ah, here's another name for you.

Jane Which one?

Derek In 1876 an American, Henry Heinz, invented tomato ketchup.

Jane That's a good one! I think we've got enough information now. Let's start writing the programme.

Unit 21a

Exercise 1

Mr Bailey Did you enjoy your trip to Denmark, Derek?

Derek Oh, yes. I enjoyed it very much.

Mrs Bailey Why did you go there?

Derek For work and pleasure. I went to Aarhus to film some of the farms there. They are very interesting and well organised. Then I went to Odense in the south to have a short holiday.

Mrs Bailey Mmm. Denmark's a very beautiful country.

Alan Do you know Denmark, Mum?

Mrs Bailey Yes, I went there to stay with my pen-friend when I was fourteen. I stayed in Copenhagen for about two weeks. It was fantastic!

Unit 21b

Exercise 1

Derek Who was the first person you saw this morning?

Jane My mother.

Derek Where was she?

Jane She was in the kitchen.

Derek Was she making your breakfast?

Jane No, she wasn't. She was standing on her head.

Derek Standing on her head?!

Jane Yes, she was doing aerobics.

Derek What were you doing when you saw her?

Jane I was walking into the kitchen to cook my breakfast!

Derek Oh I see. While you were walking into the kitchen, your mother was standing on her head!

Jane That's right.

Derek What a strange family!

Unit 21c

Exercise 4

Derek Oh dear! What a terrible morning!

Fatma Why? What happened?

Derek We were at Loch Ness.

Fatma You were filming, weren't you?

Derek Yes, that's right.

Fatma So, what was the problem?

Derek Well, while we were filming the loch, the film finished.

Fatma That's not a big problem!

Derek No, but while I was changing the film, I dropped the video camera.

Fatma Oh dear!

Derek And while I was picking up the camera, the new film fell out of it.

Fatma Oh, good heavens!

Derek And that's not all. While I was trying to put the film back in the camera, I dropped everything! The camera, the script . . . There were papers everywhere!

Fatma Then what did you do?

Derek I came back here before something else happened!

Fatma Well, everything's OK now.

Derek No, it's not. While I was driving away from the loch, I saw the monster in the car mirror.

Fatma Oh, great! Did you stop and film it?

Derek No, I only saw it for a few seconds.

Unit 22a

Exercise 2

M.O. Right, Pedro. I must ask you a few questions.

Pedro OK. Go ahead.

M.O. Now, have you ever played cricket before?

Pedro No, I haven't.

M.O. Right. No problem. Where's the form? Ah yes, here it is. Have you

ever broken your arm?
Pedro No, I haven't.
M.O. Have you ever broken your leg?
Pedro Yes, I have. About two years ago.
M.O. Uh huh. Have you ever had measles?
Pedro Measles? I don't remember. You must ask my mother.
M.O. Is she in England?
Pedro Yes, here's her phone number.
M.O. Right. I'll phone her immediately.

Unit 22b

Exercise 3

M.O. I need some information about Pedro's medical history, Mrs Alves. Pedro doesn't remember some things.
Mrs Alves No problem. I know that Pedro wants to join the Centre.
M.O. Has he ever had measles?
Mrs Alves Yes, he has.
M.O. And mumps. Has he ever had mumps?
Mrs Alves No, he hasn't but he's had chicken pox.
M.O. Ah, chicken pox. OK. Now, has he ever had scarlet fever?
Mrs Alves Oh, no he hasn't. But he's had the other childhood illnesses like rubella and whooping cough.

Unit 22c

Exercise 3

Man Question one.
Have you ever met a famous actor?
Woman Question two.
Have you ever lost your school bag?
Man Question three.
Have you ever had measles?
Woman Question four.
Has Jane ever had chicken pox?
Man Question five.
Has Tom ever cut his finger?
Woman Question six.
Has Karin ever been to Paris?
Man Question seven.
Have you ever eaten spaghetti?
Woman Question eight.
Have you ever seen an elephant?
Man Question nine.
Have you ever played water polo?
Woman Question ten.
Has Alan ever broken his leg?

Unit 23a

Exercise 2

Alan Have you seen the new *Batman* film yet, Mikis?
Mikis Yes, I have.
Karin I've already seen it too. It's very good.
Mikis Alan, have you seen the new *Superman* film?
Alan No, I haven't.
Karin I've already seen it.
Mikis Have you seen the new *Rocky* film yet, Alan?
Alan No, I haven't.
Karin I haven't either.
Mikis Well, let's go and see it now!
Alan Wait a minute. I must ask my mother.

Unit 23b

Exercise 2

Karin Grandma! What are you doing here? I thought you were in Copenhagen.
Grandma I wanted to surprise you! I'm returning to Copenhagen tomorrow.
Karin It certainly is a surprise. I haven't seen you since Christmas. What are you doing here in Brussels?
Grandma I've been to Madrid to see my sister and the plane stops in Brussels on the way back to Copenhagen.
Karin Oh, what a lovely surprise! How long have you been here?
Grandma We landed at eight o'clock this morning, so I've been in Belgium for about five hours. What time do you finish here?
Karin Now. I've finished.
Grandma Good! Let's go for a cup of coffee.
Karin Fine. And Grandpa? Did he go to Madrid with you?
Grandma No, he's at home. He doesn't like flying!

Unit 23d

Exercise 1

Fatma . . . and I want to thank you all very much. You've been fantastic! A great help to Jane, Derek and me. I don't know what to say . . . Thank you. (*applause*)

Alan Oh, that's finished. I'm really sad.
Beatrix So am I. But it's been a wonderful year.
Alan I agree. I've done so many things this year.
Beatrix So have I. I've visited England eight times.
Alan And we've met some really interesting people.
Beatrix Yes, we've met each other, people from so many different countries!
Alan And we've seen how TV programmes are made and what happens in a TV studio.
Beatrix And I've learnt a lot of English. I think in English now!
Alan What are you going to do in your spare time next year?
Beatrix That's true – with no Teen Eye we're all going to have a lot of spare time next year.
Alan My father's going to give me a movie camera for Christmas. I'm going to learn how to make films. I'm going to do a special course in photography.
Beatrix That's a good idea! Learning how to make films. I'm going to learn another language. I've always wanted to learn Russian, and next year I'm going to have extra time to study.
Alan And I'm going to start playing basketball. I've never played basketball seriously before, but I want to try.
Beatrix Yes, basketball is great fun. I'm going to learn how to play the guitar. I went to a concert of classical guitar music last month and it was beautiful.

Unit 24a

Exercise 2

Jane Have you seen Beatrix recently?
Derek No, I haven't. She hasn't been to England for about three months.
Jane And Karin? Has she been here recently?
Derek Yes, she has. She was here yesterday. She's going to come in tomorrow afternoon.
Jane Oh, good. I want to thank her for the card she sent me when I was in hospital.
Derek Beatrix is going to come to the goodbye party at the end of the week.
Jane That's great. Has Fatma finished the programme on the Olympics yet?
Derek Yes, she has.
Jane Oh, when did she finish it?
Derek Two weeks ago.
Jane Oh, what am I going to do this week?
Derek Why not get things ready for the party?

Unit 24b

Exercise 1

Fatma Hallo, Derek. This is Fatma.
Derek Hi, Fatma. What can I do for you?
Fatma There's an emergency.
Derek Oh, dear. What is it?
Fatma Peter Brown, our local Member of Parliament, has just telephoned.
Derek What's the problem?
Fatma He wants to visit the studio tomorrow.
Derek Oh no. I've just made an appointment to see the dentist tomorrow morning.
Fatma Oh, dear!
Derek Have you telephoned Jane yet?
Fatma No, I haven't. Not yet.
Derek Well, she's just gone home and she won't be here until tomorrow afternoon.
Fatma Oh, no! You must help me!
Derek Don't panic! I'll try to contact Jane tonight.

Unit 24c

Exercise 2

Fatma Where are you going this summer, Karin?

Karin I'm going to Spain with my family.

Fatma Where in Spain?

Karin To Malgrat. It's near Barcelona.

Fatma Where are you going to stay?

Karin On a campsite. We never stay in hotels.

Fatma Oh, I like camping too!

Karin Yes, it's great fun.

Fatma How long are you going to stay?

Karin Oh, two weeks. The last two weeks in August. Then back to school!

Fatma And you Mikis? Where are you going this summer?

Mikis Me? Oh, I'm going to England, to Hastings on the south coast.

Fatma What a coincidence! I'm going to Hastings too! When are you going?

Mikis The last week of July and the first two weeks of August.

Fatma Oh, what a pity! I'm going for the first week of July. Where are you going to stay?

Mikis I'm going to stay with a family and study English during the day.

Fatma Are you going on your own or with friends?

Mikis Oh, I'm going alone. I want to speak English not Greek!

Fatma I'm going alone, too. I'm going to stay in a hotel for a week and relax. The only work I'm going to do is to play golf!

Mikis Lucky you!

English coins

£1.00

50p

20p

10p

5p

1p

2p

New 50p compared with existing 50p

New £2.00